ROYAL COURT

The Royal Court Theatre presents

THE MISTRESS CONTRACT

by **Abi Morgan**

Inspired by the memoir THE MISTRESS CONTRACT by **She and He**

THE MISTRESS CONTRACT was first performed at the Royal Court Jerwood Theatre Downstairs, Sloane Square, on Thursday 30th January 2014.

THE MISTRESS CONTRACT

by **Abi Morgan**

Inspired by the memoir THE MISTRESS CONTRACT by **She and He**

Cast in alphabetical order
She **Saskia Reeves**
He **Danny Webb**

Director **Vicky Featherstone**
Designer **Merle Hensel**
Lighting Designer **Natasha Chivers**
Composer & Sound Designer **Nick Powell**
Casting Director **Julia Horan CDG**
Assistant Director **Debbie Hannan**
Production Manager **Tariq Rifaat**
Stage Manager **Michael Dennis**
Deputy Stage Manager **Julia Slienger**
Assistant Stage Manager **Sarah Coates**
Stage Management Work Placement **Kit Fordham**
Costume Supervisor **Jackie Orton**
Dialect Coach **Penny Dyer**
Set built by **Miraculous Engineering**
Set painted by **Kerry Jarret**
Scenic elements modelled by **Luca Crestani**
Cyclorama printed by **Prompt Side**
Digital Artist **Emma Pile**

The Royal Court and Stage Management wish to thank the following for their help with this production: Paul Gillieron at Gillieron Scott Acoustic, The Cactus Shop, Mike Hall at Dundee Rep, Keir Bosley, Heidi Mulvey at Cambridge University Press, James Lewis at HarperCollins UK, Thomas Walker at signature-gifts.co.uk, Jake Fordham, Random House, Oberon, Margaret at YMCA King's Road.

THE COMPANY

ABI MORGAN (Writer)

THEATRE INCLUDES: Skinned (Royal Exchange, Manchester); Splendour, Tiny Dynamite, Sleeping Around (Paines Plough); Lovesong (Frantic Assembly); Tender (Hampstead); Fugee (National); 27 (National Theatre of Scotland).

TELEVISION INCLUDES; My Fragile Heart, Murder, Sex Traffic, Tsunami – The Aftermath, White Girl, Royal Wedding, Birdsong, The Hour.

FILM INCLUDES: The Invisible Woman, Suffragette, The Iron Lady, Shame, Brick Lane.

NATASHA CHIVERS (Lighting Designer)

FOR THE ROYAL COURT: Gastronauts, The Djinns of Eidgah, That Face (&West End).

OTHER THEATRE INCLUDES: Othello, Pool (No Water), Peepshow, Tiny Dynamite, Hymns, Sell-Out (Frantic Assembly); Macbeth (Tramway/Lincoln Centre Festival); Happy Days (Sheffield Crucible Studio); The Radicalisation of Bradley Manning (National Theatre of Wales); The Wheel (Traverse/National Theatre of Scotland); 27 (Lyceum, Edinburgh/National Theatre of Scotland); The Motor Show (Brighton Festival/GDIF); Cinderella, Love (Lyric Hammersmith); The Glass Cage (Theatre Royal Northampton); Statement of Regret (National); Beyond Belief (Legs on the Wall); The Wolves in the Walls (Improbable/National Theatre of Scotland); Mercury Fur (Paines Plough/Plymouth Drum); Pyrenees (Paines Plough/Tron); Small Things (Paines Plough); The Lizzie Play (National Tour/Hong Kong Festival); The Straits (Hampstead/East 59 East); The Kindness of Strangers (Liverpool Everyman); Home (Glasgow) (National Theatre of Scotland); Run! (The Queen's House); Palace Dreams (Crystal Palace); Renaissance (Three Mills Island).

DANCE INCLUDES: Electric Hotel (Fuel/Saddler's Wells); Scattered (Motionhouse); Electric Counterpoint (Royal Opera House); Ballet for the People (Royal Festival Hall); Encore (Sadler's Wells/Tour).

OPERA INCLUDES: Zaide (Sadler's Wells/Tour); Trouble in Tahiti, Mahagonny Songspiel (The Opera Group).

PENNY DYER (Dialect Coach)

FOR THE ROYAL COURT: Circle Mirror Transformation, The Low Road, Choir Boy, In Basildon, Posh (& West End), Clybourne Park (& West End), The Faith Machine, The Girlfriend Experience, Chicken Soup with Barley, Aunt Dan and Lemon, The Fever, Tusk Tusk, Wig Out! The Pride, Now or Later, The Vertical Hour, Redundant, Plasticine, Spinning into Butter, Fireface, Other People, Mojo.

OTHER THEATRE INCLUDES: Henry V, Midsummer Night's Dream, The Cripple of Inishmaan, Peter & Alice, Privates on Parade (Michael Grandage Company); This House, Blood & Gifts (National); Sweet Bird of Youth, Hedda Gabler, Speed-the-Plow (Old Vic); The Commitments, The Book of Mormon, Abigail's Party, Absent Friends, Legally Blond, Long Day's Journey into Night (West End); Desire Under the Elms, Saved, Spring Awakening (Lyric, Hammersmith); Good People, Rupture Blister Burn, Longing, 55 Days (Hampstead); Julius Caesar (RSC); Reasons to Be Pretty, A Delicate Balance, Becky Shaw (Almeida); The Resistible Rise of Arturo Ui (CFT/West End); Kiss Me, Kate (CFT/Old Vic); Roots, The Promise, Making Noise Quietly, Salt, Root & Roe, Inadmissible Evidence, Anna Christie, The 25th Annual Putnam County Spelling Bee, Passion, A Streetcar Named Desire, Parade, Piaf, Frost/Nixon (Donmar); How To Succeed In Business (Broadway).

TELEVISION INCLUDES: Tubby & Enid, Tommy Cooper, The Great Train Robbery, The Girl, Mrs Biggs, The Job Lot, The Café, The Slap, Downton Abbey, Gracie, Small Island, Margaret, Most Sincerely, Fantabuloso, The Deal.

FILM INCLUDES: Pride, Philomena, Sunshine on Leith, The Double, Kill Your Darlings, My Week with Marilyn, Tamara Drewe, Nowhere Boy, Cheri, The Damned United, The Queen, Frost/Nixon, Infamous, Dirty Pretty Things, Ladies in Lavender, Elizabeth.

VICKY FEATHERSTONE (Director)

FOR THE ROYAL COURT: The Ritual Slaughter of Gorge Mastromas; Talk Show, Untitled Matriarch Play, The President Has Come to See You (Open Court Weekly Rep).

OTHER THEATRE INCLUDES: Enquirer (co-director), Appointment with The Wicker Man, 27, The Wheel, Somersaults, Wall of Death: A Way of Life (co-director), The Miracle Man, Empty, Long Gone Lonesome (National Theatre of Scotland); Cockroach (National Theatre of Scotland/Traverse); 356 (National Theatre of Scotland/Edinburgh International Festival); Mary Stuart (NTS/Citizens/Glasgow/Royal Lyceum); The Wolves in the Walls (co-director) (NTS/Tramway/Lyric/UK Tour/New Victory, New York); The Small Things, Pyrenees, On Blindness, The Drowned World, Tiny Dynamite, Crazy Gary's Mobile Disco, Splendour, Riddance, The Cosmonaut's Last Message to the Woman He Once Loved in the Former Soviet Union, Crave (Paines Plough).

CREATED FOR TELEVISION: Where the Heart Is, Silent Witness.

Vicky was Artistic Director of Paines Plough 1997-2005 and Artistic Director of The National Theatre of Scotland 2005-2012.

Vicky is the Artistic Director of the Royal Court.

DEBBIE HANNAN (Assistant Director)

AS DIRECTOR, FOR THE ROYAL COURT: Peckham: The Soap Opera (co-director).

AS DIRECTOR, OTHER THEATRE INCLUDES: Notes from the Underground (Citizens); Panorama, Roses Are Dead, You Cannot Call it Love (Arches); Yellow Pears (Swept Up); liberty, equality, fraternity (Tron/Traverse); Grimm Tales, Nights at the Circus (Paradok).

AS ASSISTANT DIRECTOR, THEATRE INCLUDES: A Doll's House, Enquirer (National Theatre of Scotland/Lyceum); The Maids, Beauty & the Beast (Citizens); Kurt Weill: Double Bill (Scottish Opera); War of the Roses Trilogy (Bard in the Botanics); Hamlet (Globe Education).

Debbie is Trainee Director at the Royal Court.

MERLE HENSEL (Designer)

THEATRE INCLUDES: Protest Song (National); Macbeth (NTS/Lincoln Centre/Broadway); Green Snake (National Theatre of China); Shun-Kin (Theatre de Complicite); 27, The Wheel, Glasgow Girls (National Theatre of Scotland); The Shawl, Parallel Elektra (Young Vic); The Girls of Slender Means (Stellar Quines); Diener Zweier Herren (Schlosstheatre Vienna); Ippolit (Sophiensaele, Berlin/Schauspielhaus Zürich/Münchner Kammerspiele); Der Verlorene (Sophiensaele, Belin); Kupsch (Deutsches Theatre, Göttingen).

OPERA INCLUDES: Maria Stuarda (Vereinigte Bühnen, Mönchengladbach/Krefeld); Der Vetter Aus Dingsda (Oper Graz); Lunatics (Kunstfest Weimar); Münchausen, Herr Der Lugen (Neuköllner Oper, Berlin).

DANCE INCLUDES: Sun, Political Mother (Hofesh Schecter); Lovesong (Frantic Assembly); James Son of James, The Bull, The Flowerbed (Fabulous Beast Dance Theatre); Justitia, Park (Jasmin Vardimon Dance Company); Human Shadows (Underground7/Place Prize).

FILM INCLUDES: Moriturite Te Salutant, Baby.

NICK POWELL (Composer & Sound Designer)

FOR THE ROYAL COURT: The Ritual Slaughter of Gorge Mastromas, Collaboration (Open Court), Talk Show (Open Court Weekly Rep), Narrative, Get Santa! (co-creator), The Vertical Hour, The Priory, Relocated.

AS COMPOSER/SOUND DESIGNER, OTHER THEATRE INCLUDES: Bank On It (Theatre Rites); Othello (National); A Life of Galileo, Richard III, Dunsinane, The Drunks, God in Ruins (RSC); 'Tis Pity She's A Whore (Cheek By Jowl); The Danton Affair (Stadsteatern, Gothenburg); 27, The Wheel, The Wonderful World of Dissocia (National Theatre of Scotland); Dunsinane (NTS/RSC/UK tour); Lord of the Flies, The Crucible (Regent's Park); Falstaff, Urtain, Marat-Sade (Spanish National Theatre); Paradise (Rhur Triennale/Theatre Rites); Penumbra, Tito Andronico (Animalario, Madrid); Panic (Improbable); The Family Reunion (Donmar); Bonheur (Comedie Française); Realism (National Theatre of Scotland/Edinburgh International Festival); The Wolves in the Walls (National Theatre of Scotland/Improbable).

AS SOUND DESIGNER, THEATRE INCLUDES: Wolf Hall, Bring Up the Bodies (RSC).

AWARDS INCLUDE: Animalario Award for Best Musical Composition for Scenic Arts Premios Max (Urtain).

Nick also writes music extensively for TV & film. He is half of OSKAR, who have released two albums and produced installations for the V&A and CCA, as well as written live soundtracks for Prada in Milan.

SASKIA REEVES (She)

FOR THE ROYAL COURT: The Woman Before, King Lear, Ice Cream.

OTHER THEATRE INCLUDES: Hello & Goodbye (Trafalgar Studios); A Disappearing Number (Complicite); Orpheus Descending (Donmar); Darker Face of Earth (National); Much Ado About Nothing, Man of Mode, A Midsummer Night's Dream (Cheek By Jowl); Playhouse Creatures (Old Vic); Sweet Panic, Smelling a Rat (Hampstead); A Woman Killed with Kindness, 'Tis Pity She's a Whore, Two Gentlemen of Verona, The Virtuoso (RSC); Separation (Hampstead/Comedy); Twelfth Night (Royal Exchange, Manchester); Who's Afraid of Virginia Woolf?, Measure for Measure (Young Vic); Metamorphosis (Mermaid); Infidelities (Lyric); The Attractions (Soho Poly).

TELEVISION INCLUDES: From There to Here, NTSF:SF:SUV, Vera, One Night, The Sisters, Luther, Wallander, Canoe Man, Red Riding 1983, Afterlife, Christmas Carol, Plotlands, Island at War, In My Defence, Antonia & Jane, Children Crossing, Metamorphosis.

FILM INCLUDES: The Cycling Project, Turks & Caicos, Mind Scape, Nymphomaniac, Page 8, Me & Orson Welles, The Tesseract, Heart, Different for Girls, Butterfly Kiss, I.D., Traps, The Bridge, Close My Eyes, December Bride.

DANNY WEBB (He)

FOR THE ROYAL COURT: Circle Mirror Transformation, The Witness, Chicken Soup With Barley, Piano Forte, Trade, Blue Bird, Search & Destroy, Serious Money (& Broadway), Carnival War A Go Hot.

OTHER THEATRE INCLUDES: 13, The Gardens of England, As I Lay Dying, Murderers (National); Blasted, Progress (Lyric, Hammersmith); The Ditch (Hightide); The Philanthropist (Donmar); The Green Man (Plymouth Drum/Bush); Richard III (Crucible/Tour); Art, Popcorn, Death & the Maiden (West End); Goldhawk Road, The Nest, California Dog Fight (Bush); Dead Funny (Hampstead/West End); Back up the Hearse (Hampstead); The Pool of Bethesda (Orange Tree); Hamlet (Old Vic); Night Must Fall (Greenwich).

TELEVISION INCLUDES: Lightfields, Above Suspicion, Endeavour, Sherlock, Death In Paradise, Being Human, Tucker, Holby City, Midsomer Murders, Hustle, Landgirls, The Bill, Trinity, Britannia High, Casualty, Most Sincerely, New Tricks, Lark Rise to Candleford, Honest, Bloodlines, Miss Marple, The Bill, The Rise & Fall of Rome, Doctor Who, The Inspector Lynley Mysteries, Nostradamus, Totally Frank, Lewis, Heartbeat, A Touch of Frost, Silent Witness, Waking the Dead, My Family, Uncle Adolf, Murder in Suburbia, Dogma, Pepys, Life Begins, Murder Squad, Henry VIII, Cutting It, The Hound of the Baskervilles, Torch, Outside the Rules, Shackleton, McCready & Daughter, Take Me, The Knock, Harbour Lights, Dalziel & Pascoe, Frenchman's Creek, Venus Hunters, The Jump, Out Of Hours, 2.4 Children, The Cleopatra Files, Disaster at the Mall, King Of Chaos, A Perfect State, True Tilda, Sharman, Murder Most Horrid, Mrs Hartley & the Growth Centre, Our Friends In The North, Cardiac Arrest, A Woman's Guide To Adultery, Comics, Head Hunters, Poirot, Tales of Sherwood Forest, Intimate Contact.

FILM INCLUDES: A Little Chaos, Iron Clad 2, Locke, Hummingbird, The Arbor, Visiting Hours, The Courageous Heart of Irena Sendler, Valkyrie, The Harvester, The Aryan Couple, Stealing Lives, The Upside of Anger, Family Business, Shiner, In The Name Of Love, Still Crazy, Love & Death On Long Island, True Blue, Alien III, Robin Hood, Henry V, Defence of the Realm, The Kid & the Green Baize Vampire, The Year of the Quiet Sun, The Unapproachable, No Exit.

THE ENGLISH STAGE COMPANY AT THE ROYAL COURT THEATRE

photo: Stephen Cummiskey

'For me the theatre is really a religion or way of life. You must decide what you feel the world is about and what you want to say about it, so that everything in the theatre you work in is saying the same thing ... A theatre must have a recognisable attitude. It will have one, whether you like it or not.'

George Devine, first artistic director of the English Stage Company: notes for an unwritten book.

As Britain's leading national company dedicated to new work, the Royal Court Theatre produces new plays of the highest quality, working with writers from all backgrounds, and addressing the problems and possibilities of our time.

"The Royal Court has been at the centre of British cultural life for the past 50 years, an engine room for new writing and constantly transforming the theatrical culture." Stephen Daldry

Since its foundation in 1956, the Royal Court has presented premieres by almost every leading contemporary British playwright, from John Osborne's Look Back in Anger to Caryl Churchill's A Number and Tom Stoppard's Rock 'n' Roll. Just some of the other writers to have chosen the Royal Court to premiere their work include Edward Albee, John Arden, Richard Bean, Samuel Beckett, Edward Bond, Leo Butler, Jez Butterworth, Martin Crimp, Ariel Dorfman, Stella Feehily, Christopher Hampton, David Hare, Eugène Ionesco, Ann Jellicoe, Terry Johnson, Sarah Kane, David Mamet, Martin McDonagh, Conor McPherson, Joe Penhall, Lucy Prebble, Mark Ravenhill, Simon Stephens, Wole Soyinka, Polly Stenham, David Storey, Debbie Tucker Green, Arnold Wesker and Roy Williams.

"It is risky to miss a production there." Financial Times

In addition to its full-scale productions, the Royal Court also facilitates international work at a grass-roots level, developing exchanges which bring young writers to Britain and sending British writers, actors and directors to work with artists around the world. The research and play development arm of the Royal Court Theatre, The Studio, finds the most exciting and diverse range of new voices in the UK. The Studio runs play-writing groups including the Young Writers Programme, Critical Mass for Black, Asian and minority ethnic writers and the biennial Young Writers Festival. For further information, go to www.royalcourttheatre.com/playwriting/the-studio.

Supported by
**ARTS COUNCIL
ENGLAND**

New Season
Until Aug 2014

Jerwood Theatre Downstairs

3 Apr – 24 May
Birdland
By Simon Stephens
Cast includes: Alex Price, Andrew Scott
A piercing new play looking at
empathy, money and fame.

13 Jun – 5 Jul
Adler & Gibb
By Tim Crouch
Tells the story of a raid – on a house,
a life, a reality and a legacy.

17 Jul – 9 Aug
Co-produced with Headlong
The Nether
By Jennifer Haley
An intricate crime drama and
haunting sci-fi thriller.

West End Duchess Theatre
3 – 15 Feb

The Royal Court Theatre and Mighty Mouth present
Not I/Footfalls/Rockaby
By Samuel Beckett
The sold out show, performed by Lisa Dwan
and directed by Walter Asmus, transfers to
the Duchess Theatre in the West End for a
limited run at Royal Court prices.

£25, £20, £12 (£1 booking fee)

Jerwood Theatre Upstairs

Until 1 Mar
The Pass
By John Donnelly
Cast: Gary Carr, Lisa McGrillis,
Nico Mirallegro, Russell Tovey
An agile new story about sex, fame,
and how much you're willing to lose
in order to win.

27 Mar – 3 May
Co-produced with Clean Break and Royal
Exchange Theatre Manchester.
Pests
By Vivienne Franzmann
Cast: Ellie Kendrick, Sinéad Matthews
Pink loves Rolly. Rolly loves Pink.
And Pink loves getting bombed off
her face. The story of two sisters from
the same nest.
Part of the Royal Court's Jerwood New
Playwrights programme, supported by the
Jerwood Charitable Foundation.

11 – 28 June
Co-produced with Birmingham Repertory Theatre
Khandan (Family)
By Gurpreet Kaur Bhatti
A warm and funny play about
tradition and ambition.

Innovation Partner

Flight Partner

Tickets from £10
020 7565 5000
www.royalcourttheatre.com
 royalcourt theroyalcourttheatre

ROYAL COURT SUPPORTERS

The Royal Court has significant and longstanding relationships with many organisations and individuals who provide vital support. It is this support that makes possible its unique playwriting and audience development programmes.

Coutts supports Innovation at the Royal Court. The Genesis Foundation supports the Royal Court's work with International Playwrights. Theatre Local is sponsored by Bloomberg. Alix Partners support The Big Idea at the Royal Court. The Jerwood Charitable Foundation supports emerging writers through the Jerwood New Playwrights series. The Andrew Lloyd Webber Foundation supports the Royal Court's Studio, which aims to seek out, nurture and support emerging playwrights. The Harold Pinter Playwright's Award is given annually by his widow, Lady Antonia Fraser, to support a new commission at the Royal Court.

PUBLIC FUNDING
Arts Council England, London
British Council

CHARITABLE DONATIONS
Martin Bowley Charitable Trust
Columbia Foundation Fund of the London
Community Foundation
Cowley Charitable Trust
The Dorset Foundation
The Eranda Foundation
Genesis Foundation
The Golden Bottle Trust
The Haberdashers' Company
The Idlewild Trust
Jerwood Charitable Foundation
Marina Kleinwort Trust
The Andrew Lloyd Webber Foundation
John Lyon's Charity
Clare McIntyre's Bursary
The Andrew W. Mellon Foundation
The David & Elaine Potter Foundation
Rose Foundation
The Royal College of Psychiatrists
Royal Victoria Hall Foundation
The Sackler Trust
The Sobell Foundation
John Thaw Foundation
The Vandervell Foundation
Sir Siegmund Warburg's Voluntary Settlement
The Garfield Weston Foundation

CORPORATE SUPPORTERS & SPONSORS
AKA
Alix Partners
American Airlines
BBC
Bloomberg

Café Colbert
Coutts
Fever-Tree
Kudos Film & Television
MAC
Moët & Chandon
Quintessentially Vodka
Smythson of Bond Street
White Light Ltd

BUSINESS ASSOCIATES, MEMBERS & BENEFACTORS
Annoushka
Auerbach & Steele Opticians
Bank of America Merrill Lynch
Byfield Consultancy
Capital MSL
Cream
Lazard
Vanity Fair
Waterman Group

DEVELOPMENT ADVOCATES
John Ayton MBE
Elizabeth Bandeen
Kinvara Balfour
Anthony Burton CBE
Piers Butler
Sindy Caplan
Sarah Chappatte
Cas Donald (Vice Chair)
Celeste Fenichel
Emma Marsh (Chair)
Deborah Shaw Marquardt (Vice Chair)
Tom Siebens
Sian Westerman
Daniel Winterfeldt

 Supported by
ARTS COUNCIL ENGLAND

Innovation Partner

INDIVIDUAL MEMBERS

MAJOR DONORS
Anonymous
Eric Abraham
Ray Barrell & Ursula Van Almsick
Cas Donald
Lydia & Manfred Gorvy
Richard & Marcia Grand
Jack & Linda Keenan
Adam Kenwright
Mandeep Manku
Miles Morland
Mr & Mrs Sandy Orr
NoraLee & Jon Sedmak
Deborah Shaw & Stephen Marquardt
Jan & Michael Topham
Monica B Voldstad

MOVER-SHAKERS
Anonymous
Christine Collins
Jordan Cook
Mr & Mrs Roderick Jack
Duncan Matthews QC
Mr & Mrs Timothy D Proctor
Ian & Carol Sellars

BOUNDARY-BREAKERS
Katie Bradford
Piers & Melanie Gibson
David Harding
Madeleine Hodgkin
Philip & Joan Kingsley
Emma Marsh
Edgar & Judith Wallner
Mr & Mrs Nick Wheeler

GROUNDBREAKERS
Anonymous
Allen Appen & Jane Wiest
Moira Andreae
Mr & Mrs Simon Andrews
Nick Archdale
Charlotte Asprey
Jane Attias
Elizabeth & Adam Bandeen
Michael Bennett
Dr Kate Best
Sarah & David Blomfield
Stan & Val Bond
Neil & Sarah Brener
Deborah Brett
Mr & Mrs William Broeksmit
Joanna Buckenham
Lois Moore & Nigel Burridge
Louise Burton
Clive & Helena Butler

Piers Butler
Sindy & Jonathan Caplan
Gavin & Lesley Casey
Sarah & Philippe Chappatte
Tim & Caroline Clark
Carole & Neville Conrad
Andrea & Anthony Coombs
Clyde Cooper
Ian & Caroline Cormack
Mr & Mrs Cross
Andrew & Amanda Cryer
Alison Davies
Roger & Alison De Haan
Matthew Dean
Polly Devlin OBE
Rob & Cherry Dickins
Sophie Diedrichs-Cox
Denise & Randolph Dumas
Robyn Durie
Glenn & Phyllida Earle
The Edwin Fox Foundation
Lisa Erikson & Edward Ocampo
Mark & Sarah Evans
Celeste & Peter Fenichel
Margy Fenwick
Beverley Gee
Nick & Julie Gould
Lord & Lady Grabiner
Jill Hackel & Andrzej Zarzycki
Carol Hall
Stephen & Jennifer Harper
Mr & Mrs Sam Haubold
Gordon & Brette Holmes
Kate Hudspeth
Damien Hyland
Suzie & David Hyman
Melanie J. Johnson
Nicholas Jones
Dr Evi Kaplanis
David P Kaskel & Christopher A Teano
Vincent & Amanda Keaveny
Peter & Maria Kellner
Nicola Kerr
Steve Kingshott
Mr & Mrs Pawel Kisielewski
Mr & Mrs David & Sarah Kowitz
Rosemary Leith
Daisy & Richard Littler
Kathryn Ludlow
Beatrice & James Lupton CBE

Suzanne Mackie
Dr Ekaterina Malievskaia & George Goldsmith
Christopher Marek Rencki
Mrs Janet Martin
Andrew McIver
Barbara Minto
Takehito Mitsui
Angelie Moledina
Ann & Gavin Neath CBE
Clive & Annie Norton
Georgia Oetker
James Orme-Smith
Mr & Mrs Guy Paterson
Sir William & Lady Vanessa Patey
Andrea & Hilary Ponti
Annie & Preben Prebensen
Wendy & Philip Press
Julie Ritter
Paul & Gill Robinson
Andrew & Ariana Rodger
Corinne Rooney
William & Hilary Russell
Julie & Bill Ryan
Sally & Anthony Salz
Bhags Sharma
The Michael & Melanie Sherwood Charitable Foundation
Tom Siebens & Mimi Parsons
Andy Simpkin
Anthony Simpson & Susan Boster
Andrea Sinclair & Serge Kremer
Paul & Rita Skinner
Mr & Mrs RAH Smart
Brian Smith
Barbara Soper
Saadi & Zeina Soudavar
Sue St Johns
The Ulrich Family
Amanda Vail
Constanze Von Unruh
Ian & Victoria Watson & The Watson Foundation
Jens Smith Wergeland
Matthew & Sian Westerman
Mrs Alexandra Whiley
Anne-Marie Williams
Sir Robert & Lady Wilson
Mr Daniel Winterfeldt & Mr Jonathan Leonhart
Katherine & Michael Yates

With thanks to our Friends, Stage-Taker and Ice-Breaker members whose support we greatly appreciate.

Make a Donation

By making a donation to the Royal Court you can help us to respond to new and established playwrights, and supply them with the time, resources and environment to follow their imagination and exceed their potential.

Help us to make the Royal Court the renowned international success that it is.

To make a donation to the Royal Court, please:
Call Anna Sampson on 020 7565 5049
Email annasampson@royalcourttheatre.com
Visit royalcourttheatre.com/support-us/make-a-donation

Thank you in advance for supporting our work and changing theatre forever.

www.royalcourttheatre.com

The English Stage Company at the Royal Court Theatre is a registered charity (No. 231242).

Photo: John Haynes

THE MISTRESS CONTRACT

Abi Morgan

THE MISTRESS CONTRACT

Inspired by the memoir
The Mistress Contract **by She and He**

OBERON BOOKS
LONDON

WWW.OBERONBOOKS.COM

The Mistress Contract was first published in the United Kingdom in 2013 by Serpent's Tail, an imprint of Profile Books Ltd.

This adaptation first published in 2014 by Oberon Books Ltd
521 Caledonian Road, London N7 9RH
Tel: +44 (0) 20 7607 3637 / Fax: +44 (0) 20 7607 3629
e-mail: info@oberonbooks.com
www.oberonbooks.com

A catalogue record for this book is available from the British Library.

PB ISBN: 978-1-78319-053-9
E ISBN: 978-1-78319-552-7

Cover image by Richard Sandler

Printed, bound and converted
by CPI Group (UK) Ltd, Croydon, CR0 4YY.

Visit www.oberonbooks.com to read more about all our books and to buy them. You will also find features, author interviews and news of any author events, and you can sign up for e-newsletters so that you're always first to hear about our new releases.

For She and He

Characters

HE

[mid 50s – mid 70s]

SHE

[from early 50s – early 70s]

The play takes place in a house in West California
over 30 years from 1981 to 2010.

SCENE 1 – HOUSE

A low slung beautiful 60s house in West California. It is empty, in waiting.

A wide window, strung with a broken blind. Late afternoon sunlight scissored across the room.

It is late afternoon, 1981.

HE stands his coat still on.

SHE rummages through her handbag, in search of her cigarettes.

SHE: You know this won't work if you don't take it seriously.

>*SHE finds the cigarettes triumphant.*

HE: I can't see why you're so mad with me. I visited less than a week ago –

SHE: We went over this on the telephone –

>*SHE wavers, lighting a cigarette.*

HE: …And as I seem to remember it I made love to you all night.

SHE: That's not strictly true.

>*HE wavers.*

HE: Didn't you enjoy it?

>*SHE crosses the room, over to the window, peers through the broken blind. SHE searches for a cord at last finding it and pulls up a broken blind to reveal, a garden in need of work, and then the desert.*

SHE: It was fine.

>*SHE fiddles with a window lock. It refuses to budge.*

What d'you want? A medal?

>*SHE reaches in her handbag, pulling out a pile of books, clearly in search of something.*

9

HE: Is this your group? Is this what you discuss in your group? The inadequacies of penetration?

SHE: Oh please –

HE: What? What?

> *He peers at the clutch of books, pulled out of her bag.*

> *(Reading titles.) The Feminine Mystique* – Betty Friedan. *The Female Man* by Joanna Russ. *Woman Hating – A Radical Look at Sexuality* – Andrea Dworkin.

>> *He turns over the book, considers the photo of the author on the back cover.*

Is *she* in fact a *he*? Is that a man? Did you read all of these? Is it obligatory before you can sit with your *sisters* and decimate the men in your lives?

SHE: Oh my God you are a shit. You are a shit. You are just like *him.*

HE: We often are. Apparently. Ex-husbands. Or so my ex-wife tells me.

> *SHE stubs out her cigarette.*

SHE: Forget it… Forget it… I can see how ridiculous this is.

> *SHE shoves the books back in her bag.*

These books. These books are opening me up. These books are what got me out of my last marriage. These books are what got me here. These books are what I read when you're not around. When you're asleep.

HE: What does that mean? What do you *infer*?

SHE: We got back to the hotel room and you fell asleep. So strictly speaking you did *not* make love to me all night.

HE: That's not entirely true.

SHE: Really? When you got off the plane you were tired, tired.

HE: I drove.

SHE: …so that halfway down the freeway, you could pull out
your penis and say 'Suck me'.

HE: Ah –

SHE: What I'd been doing, what I'd been feeling, you didn't
ask. You said 'Do it'. You didn't ask me if I wanted to.

HE: And you didn't say no.

> *SHE hesitates.*

And then when we got to the hotel, I made love to you all
night.

SHE: No, when we got to the hotel, you talked and then you
went to sleep because you were so tired. Then you woke in
the middle of the night and it grazed your conscience that
maybe we should make love. So *you* did.

HE: You weren't present?

SHE: Being present didn't seem important. I didn't notice you
checking whether I was present or not. Intimacy to you is
one thing, to me another. *Is* another.

HE: Is this because I didn't stay for breakfast the next day?

> *HE laughs, moving around the house, opening cupboards,
> doors.*

You want companionship with breakfast, long walks.

SHE: You want sex.

HE: In all shapes, sizes, varieties.

SHE: Therefore an exchange between individuals can be
considered a marketplace in which individuals exchange
those things they have for those things they want.

> *They smile at one another.*

HE: Was this an idea you came up with in your group?

SHE: No. They don't know about it.

HE: I should think not. What would the sisters say to that?

> *SHE shakes her head.*

You sucked his cock? Your husband's?

SHE: Ex-husband's. *(Beat.)* Yes.

HE: And your husband before that? Your first husband's –

SHE: I did.

HE: But you didn't like it? You don't like it?

> *SHE looks at him.*

SHE: You raided the mini bar and complained that there was no cabernet. And I rang down and got you some. While you gave a lecture on existentialism and what is the *point of one's existence.* And then you asked me to suck your cock *again* and I responded by saying to you…

HE: I do remember this.

SHE: …I said 'This is my present. My present condition is, *the point of my existence* is when I am asked to suck, when it is conveyed to me –

HE: This is all making sense to me now.

SHE: …that that would be desired, my existence at that moment is to wonder why you like it so much. To wonder why I have been doing it all these years. To wonder if there is anything more useless to me and more pleasurable to you.

> *He goes to interrupt.*

Let me finish my sentence…I think in that moment… 'I wonder what my vagina is for.' And that is when you fell asleep.

> *She exits. He looks on.*

HE: *(Calling out.)* I wasn't saying being an existentialist meant being a zombie. My message…my message…was that you have a choice. And you exaggerate. Which you are prone to do. It wasn't the only thing we talked about.

She comes back, picking up her forgotten handbag.

SHE: But at the moment that it is happening, what am I suppose to do with all my thoughts? They are there. Like Camus' stranger. I am the passive recipient of a man's plans and am surrounded at such times by a feeling that I have not been consulted, that I am, in fact a nobody.

HE: Then you should be clear. Know what you want. You shouldn't pretend. You should assert. If you really want to avoid that act you should say 'This is the price of admission into my intimacy. If you want anything else, go someplace else.' Ninety-nine per cent of the time you make it so unpleasant there should be a cessation of all such activities anyway. You make it a federal case every time it occurs. You raise the issue of the vagina? I could screw you a hundred times as I have, then ask you to suck me once and you would still say 'What have I got a vagina for?'

SHE: Every man I have ever known, with one exception has asked for sucking –

HE: Now you're falling into –

SHE: Let me finish – which puts into a strange perspective all the other ways of lovemaking.

HE: When you say 'every man' do you include me in that?

SHE: So what I should really say is – 'Look my throat is too small, my taste is for celery and peanut butter, not semen and I am a nervous vomiter. It can't be the nature of your sexuality to wish to place your generative organ down my throat!'

HE: But you don't.

SHE wavers –

SHE: Intimacy to *you* is one thing, to *me* another.

> *They let the silence hang.*

I've been raising my kids, teaching my class, g*oing to my group*…as you put it and you're…you're in another state all together, doing your board meetings and monitoring your corporate income projections and making investment decisions. And reading your books, your intellectual books to appease the guilt and mindless, endless moral contradictions of what your day job is –

And I'm here, waiting. Having a whole other life, living a whole other life and yet all I really want is for you to call. And then you do and I'm here. I come at your whim. And I have nowhere to put my feminism. I am powerless in the face of you and my feminism… My Dworkin, Miller, Millet fuelled feminism is beyond tested, is annihilated by my desire for you. *(Direct to the audience.)* And these are the thoughts that dog my day. That led me to…the idea.

> *He considers.*

HE: Is this some kind of protest?

SHE: My feminism is boring to you.

HE: I haven't seen very many comedies about it.

> *SHE hesitates, goes over to the window.*

Fidelity –

SHE: *'Reduces you'.* Yes you said that. After your speech on existentialism. Or was it before I sucked your cock? This is not about fidelity.

HE: I want sex you want –

SHE: I want sex too. And breakfasts and walks.

HE: Breakfast and walks always seem like a good postlude. There's nothing wrong with that.

SHE: But the only way of holding you to the walks is to delay the sex. The sex is all that is important to you.

HE: You perceive sex as your only bargaining chip – not your wit, your charm, your conversation?

SHE: You value my wit more than you value sex?

He hesitates –

HE: *(Direct to audience.)* If you read about men who were obviously fascinating personalities, you will usually find a female that fascinated them.

SHE: It's a simple question.

HE: *(Direct to audience.)* Napoleon, Caesar, Pompey, Roosevelt, Kennedy, Johnson. All men of action… All had fascinating women –

SHE: *(Direct to audience.)* All went elsewhere.

She turns back to him.

Sometimes when you don't call I call you at your house and sometimes a woman answers. I'd say from the accent she was from Seattle.

HE: You are asking me to be exclusive.

SHE: That is not what I am saying.

HE: You are asking me to be exclusive.

SHE laughs, shakes her head.

SHE: What do you value more – my wit or sex?

HE: It's not you. It's just not what I want.

SHE: Again, you still haven't answered my question.

HE looks at her.

OK. I'll put it another way. When you leave, you get on your plane and you pick up your car and you drive to

15

your house. Which I have never seen. And perhaps our lady from Seattle is waiting for you as you come through arrivals. And perhaps you get into a car with her. And she is sitting next to you in the passenger seat. And as you pull out of the airport lot you say 'Suck my cock'. 'Do it'. And she sucks it.?

> *Silence.*

Does she?

HE: Yes.

> *She laughs –*

And she doesn't complain. She likes the taste.

SHE: She tells you that?

HE: I know –

SHE: She tells you that?

> *HE wavers.*

No I expect you're too busy being blinded by her wit and conversation to hear.

HE: No, her mouth is too full to speak.

> *SHE looks at him.*

SHE: Sally's right. I shouldn't be doing this.

HE: So you did talk to your *sisters.*

SHE: She's in my group.

HE: And will you entertain Sally and Linda and Jim… Isn't one of them called Jim…will you entertain Jim and your sisters here?

SHE: You didn't take this seriously at all.

> *HE takes out a contract and puts it down on the table between the two of them.*

Did you even read it? Did you understand it?

HE: I read it as it came through on the fax. I read it twice. I called you as soon as it arrived. As soon as I had read it. I took it very seriously. What man wouldn't take it seriously? What man would ignore an offer like that?

>*Silence.*

Yes I read it.

>*Silence.*

Yes I understood it.

SHE: I won't be indebted. It has be on the contracts terms –

HE: It's the greatest offer I've ever received.

SHE: You haven't thought about it. I can tell you haven't thought about it.

HE: We're here aren't we?

>*They look at one another.*

Does this not show you I've taken it seriously? Does this not show you I have thought about it?

>*She takes in the house, looks around a little more.*

I hope it's to your liking.

SHE: The view's –

>*They look at the view –*

HE: Expensive.

>*SHE looks at him.*

But the drive's good. The airport's easy from here. So when I fly in –

>*SHE moves around the room, running a finger along a shelf, taking in the space.*

…and you pick me up, the drive won't take as long.

SHE: That shouldn't be a problem. You come pretty quick.

> *HE hesitates – laughs.*

HE: The question is have you taken this seriously?

SHE: I proposed this so you don't need to ask how seriously I have thought about it. I've been trying it out in my head ever since I sent it. The idea of it. The word – *Mistress.*

HE: And?

SHE: The alternative… It's miserable. I'm miserable… It's making me miserable. You're making me miserable.

> *SHE laughs, throws her hands up in the air. SHE reaches for her bag, rifles through it, finds her cigarettes. SHE opens them, offers them. He takes one. They light up, smoke. SHE walks over to the window.*

Is there a key for this thing?

> *HE nods, searches through his pockets, handing over keys. SHE takes it, unlocks the glass, sliding it open. A breeze coming in.*

I'm teaching some poor fifth grader, reassuring him, it doesn't matter, this is the alternative, we don't do grades here and all he really wants to know is did he get an A+ for that and I say *That's not the point, sweetie. We're not that kind of school.* And someone always wants something from me. And my daughter's home with some crisis… And my sons… Well they're nearly grown up now… But when they are home… They always want something…

And then we have that fight. And I think I need to be paid for this.

I consider myself a feminist. I consider myself equal to you but in sex we're just not. So this way you pay me what I am owed. What I feel I am owed and in return you get what you are owed. This is 'the price of admission into my intimacy'.

They look at one another.

I watch my children. Girls are bad but boys… They are the worse. And now those boys are becoming men… Mine come home for the weekend and they do nothing… And there is nothing I can do.

SHE draws on her cigarette. Exhales.

I'm just sending them out into the world.

SHE draws on her cigarette. Exhales.

To go and do what they do best. Go and be men.

SHE draws on her cigarette. Exhales.

God help their girlfriends.

SHE stubs out her cigarette.

So we had that fight and I just put down the phone and I paced around for a while then I sat in front of the typewriter and it just came to me… It just sort of poured out. I faxed it before I could change my mind.

SHE stops, seeing the pool beyond.

It's got a pool?

HE: Yes. And a Yucca –

SHE: Oh yeah.

HE: It'll dry out so you'll need to water it.

SHE looks at him.

SHE: I know how to water a plant.

HE shakes his head.

HE: We see one another …two…three times a month –

SHE: If I'm lucky.

HE: We speak on the phone… Every couple of days at least.

SHE: That's not what I'm saying.

HE: You're getting angry again.

SHE: I'm not. Really I'm not. And I'm not angry with you…
I'm not… That's not what this is… I don't want to be a
wife. I don't want marriage. I've done that before. That's
not what this is about. It's the opposite of what this is
about. You do see that?

> *SHE looks at him.*

And I am not asking for fidelity?

HE: Right.

SHE: Because we know you don't do that.

HE: And – ?

SHE: You don't ask that question of me either. When I am with
you I am yours and when I'm not I can be with whoever I
want to be. Do whatever I want to do. Do you hear me?

HE: Loud and clear.

> *Silence.*

What did you think when I said yes?

SHE: I felt soaringly happy…I feel soaringly happy at this
whole antic. Seeing it in bold…as I typed it. You know
if you look at the word…really look at the word…
CONTRACT. It's so definite… So permanent… It's
a commitment. I'm surprised you were even wiling to
consider it. But then you are a practical man. You've
watched me battle my ex through the courtrooms. So
many recriminations. Having my sanity questioned.
Whether I could even look after my kids. Almost losing
everything. I mean you've seen that… You watched me go
through that… This way. What I want and what I can give
are clear –

HE: You know it doesn't entirely stand up in a court of law.

SHE: Does a marriage contract? Vows are breakable. I broke them. You broke them… But then I never saw marriage as a business deal. This way – the terms and conditions are clear?

HE: Absolutely. I find them very clear.

> *HE pulls a faxed contract out of his back pocket.*

Though I've had a lawyer go over it.

> *SHE wavers.*

As you say this *is* a business deal. I wouldn't sign anything without getting my lawyer to go over it first. Do you mind – ?

> *SHE shakes her head. HE reads –*

1] This contract is for mistress services to be carried out by Ms… That's you for Mr… That's me.

2] The compensation for these services shall be at whatever amount is required to provide Ms…you…tasteful accommodations to her liking –

> *He gestures to the surroundings.*

…Together with expenses accrued in the normal course of her activities.

SHE: This won't be excessive.

HE: Thank you.

SHE: As long as we are clear what we both get out of it.

HE: Manage our expectations?

SHE: Exactly.

> *SHE takes in the room.*

When I was married I used to look around our house and I'd think what have I got? A couch, kids, cutlery and a man's protection. Well that's so far disappointed me. This way? I get what's expected. I expect no more. It saves on disappointment. It makes me –

SHE opens cupboards, peering in.

…less angry.

HE: You hope.

SHE: It's an experiment. Who knows if it will work? Isn't that the point of an experiment? The mere act of trying is the point. If it fails…? That's just the natural conclusion. At least it's real. This has to be real. It's a scheme that I hope will allow me freedom. *Us* both freedom.

HE: Yes.

SHE: That's what I hope… In giving it away… In just throwing away all of it… All that I've believed in… All the literature I have supported… My feminism… In going against my feminism –

HE: Your sisters –

SHE: There's that facetiousness again.

HE: …You can go to your meetings, express rage with your sisters and know if you are being screwed at least you are being paid.

SHE: In paying me for all that I have previously done… thought I have done out of love…to be paid for all of that…it's liberating…I hope it will be liberating.

And you are a lot richer than you can make use of.

So I'm yours unless indisposed or travelling.

The kids are nearly flown. I have to look after myself now. And I am penniless. This is an answer.

HE: If it's just about money… I can give you money.

SHE hesitates.

SHE: One answer.

SHE gestures to the contract.

You can read on if you like.

HE nods, returns to his contract, reads.

HE: *In return for this compensation, you will provide the following mistress services a] Companionship for me when I am in the area, unless you are indisposed or travelling. b] All sexual acts engaged in when requested by me...*

HE wavers.

All sexual acts?

SHE: Yes.

HE resumes reading.

HE: *...with suspension of historical –*

HE murmurs, as if reading a part to himself.

...physical, emotional, psychological disclaimers for duration of –

HE murmurs, as if reading part to himself...

...time requested to be determined by me.

SHE reaches into her pocket and pulls out a pen, holding it out to him.

There's more.

He reads on.

For duration of agreement you become sexual property of me...

He looks up.

Then we sign.

SHE nods.

Your name's first.

HE turns searching for some suitable place to sign. HE places the contract down on a counter. SHE goes to sign it.

Shouldn't you read it before you sign?

SHE hesitates, hands the pen to him.

SHE: You go first.

HE signs.

You should date it.

HE wavers. HE goes to date it.

It's 1981.

HE wavers.

HE: I know the year.

HE finishes up, hands it to her. SHE goes to take it. HE looks at her. SHE signs it.

SHE: Thank you.

HE: You're welcome.

SHE opens her purse, about to put the contract in it.

I'd like a copy. Just for my files.

SHE: Of course.

SHE slides the contract into her bag. Then takes out a tape recorder, placing it on the table between them.

And we tape ourselves.

SHE leans over, goes to turn the tape recorder on, finger reaching for 'record.'

HE: Every conversation?

SHE leans forward fiddles with the tape, rewinds, plays.

(Recorded voice.) Every conversation?

She smiles, presses record.

SHE: Not all the time… From time to time. Reflections. Thoughts. When we meet. I want to stay engaged. It can't drift. This is an experiment, I want a record, of how it works. *If* it works.

HE: And if it doesn't? Work?

SHE: Then we'll have had some fun along the way.

They laugh, smile.

HE: I didn't bring anything to drink.

SHE: We can go out. There's that nice place, not far from the Canyon… Does great coffee in the day. *Hilary's* –

HE: I need to be in Silverlake by eight –

SHE nods, reaches for her bag, slides the tape recorder inside her bag. SHE looks out at the pool beyond.

I'll arrange for a boy to clean the pool.

SHE wavers, nods.

SHE: Thank you.

HE: For what?

SHE: For joining me in this experiment.

They look at one another – smile.

I need that drink. *(Beat.)*

SHE laughs.

HE: You know this will trap you too. You might think you can get out of it but for this to work… Habit will trap you. We'll develop behaviour patterns and you won't be able to escape.

SHE: How? There is no battle now.

HE doesn't move.

We should take the recorder with us. It might not pick up in the bar but we can try. We can find out if Reagan's dead yet.

HE: He's still on the operating table. Apparently he wouldn't let them knock him out until he knew the surgeon was a republican. I guess if you've dodged a bullet once…

SHE: God I didn't get spare tape. Remind me I must get spare –

HE: Not yet.

> *HE gently stops her, leaving the tape on.*

I don't want to go yet.

> *SHE winces – sun in her eyes.*

SHE: God that sun's bright.

> *SHE looks up, sees no blinds.*

What?

> *SHE looks at him, holds his gaze.*

OK.

> *SHE unzips his flies.*

We'll need blinds.

> *Beat.*

> *They both speak to the audience.*

(Direct to audience.) We began our recording of conversations on Saturday after buying a Sony tape recorder that could fit in my purse. I felt strengthened by the device. We tried it first in the bar, and it sucked up our words in spite of a speaker on the wall nearby, and we continued over dinner.

HE: *(Direct to audience.)* Our words gradually become slurred with wine, and often our mouths were full.

SHE: *(Direct to audience.)* What emerges –

HE: *(Direct to audience.)* …when you listen to the tapes is –

SHE: *(Direct to audience.)* He's fluent, pedantic, complex compound, archaically eloquent, long-winded, and occasionally – when he switches to simple diction – comical. He dominates the conversation by his flow –

HE: *(Direct to audience.)* …but it is apparent that the subject interests me, that I have –

SHE: *(Direct to audience.)* …many thoughts on – male-female boundaries and wishes to understand.

HE: *(Direct to audience.)* I listen.

SHE: (Direct to audience.) I am much less skilled at speaking and confine myself to that which I feel or know, or think I know. Several times I confess to feeling confused about where we are going and say so. We get back on target.

> *She smiles.*

Did I say this was 1981?

> *Blackout.*

SCENE 2 – BED

The same house. A bed. SHE and HE caught in a tangle of sheets, post coital watching TV – The Invasion of Grenada mid report. A few more books on the shelves. Beyond the same view of the desert. There is a present, half open on the side table. His briefcase stands by the door.

It is dusk, 1983.

HE gets up, crosses the room to the bathroom, to pee.

SHE: *(Calling out to him.)* We must be the most screwed up country in the solar system. If we're not invading countries then we have kooks trying to murder us at home.

> *SHE sits down watching the TV until –*

Last weekend I couldn't take a walk along the Canyon because the police stopped my car searching for that killer. Do you know how many women he has raped and murdered now? That other fuck… What was his name? Singleton. That nut pleaded to the judge that the girl was walking around alone, was not dressed properly, and she made overtures toward him.

HE: What else was he to do? Cut her arms of course.

SHE: Fourteen years for rape, sodomy –

HE: This is very morbid.

SHE: My children tell me this also.

HE: Then listen to them.

SHE: How can I listen to them?

> *SHE leans over, flicks the TV off.*

A has gone hitchhiking with a friend again this weekend.

> *HE returns, climbs back into bed.*

HE: What does that have to do with what we were talking about?

SHE: What I was saying… What I was saying was.

> *The click of the tape.*

Damn. The tape's run out.

> *SHE points to a drawer.*

New tape.

HE: Where?

SHE: Side drawer.

> *SHE rewinds the tape, plays. Her voice just audible –*

SHE: *(Recorded voice.)* Sex, underneath all the love, has a basic element of violence. It is a taking. A man ultimately penetrates, has the physical –

> *HE hands her the tape. SHE changes the tape, puts in a new tape and presses record. SHE writes on the old tape box, and then slides it with the old tape onto a shelf.*

HE: That doesn't make me a rapist. That doesn't make me some kook reaching for my gun.

> *A splashing coming from the pool.*

SHE: Did you ever discuss sex with your wife…sorry ex-wife. With L?

HE: I can't remember.

SHE: You must have talked sometimes.

HE: Hardly ever. Hardly ever with L.

SHE: Never.

HE: I don't remember.

> *HE stands, reaching for his robe, and peers through the blind. HE throws a half wave.*

What happened to Julio?

SHE: Varicose vein removal. That's his cousin.

HE: You know he wouldn't have to clear leaves if you just pulled the cover over from time to time.

>SHE *reaches for a cup of coffee, drinks, hands it to him.*

SHE: You never talked about sex with your wife because men make it difficult for women to talk about sex… About what they want. In talking about it… I don't know… They… men…feel it reduces them… No…it threatens a man's power.

HE: That's not true.

>*HE drinks.*

I have talked about sex with women.

SHE: Just not with your wife?

HE: With women I have been involved with. Women I have not had children with.

SHE: Because those women have remained unencumbered.

HE: Yes in a way.

SHE: And when they were not available… You turned to porn?

HE: Sometimes. Yes. At times yes.

SHE: Impossible fantasy.

>*SHE nods, heads into the bathroom.*

HE: You like to treat males more as abstractions which you endow with various characteristics but are relatively indifferent to who they actually are.

>*SHE comes out, holding a bottle of pills.*

SHE: That's probably not true.

>*SHE takes a couple, drinks her coffee, slides the pill bottle down on the side by her bed.*

Incidentally you have 15 minutes. My group are coming over. We have our book discussion. Sally's leading. *(Pointing to tape recorder.)* Are we definitely on?

> *She checks the tape.*

HE: You all generalise. You categorise. Men are this. Women are that. You make assumptions about a man's…my… needs. But you…you…you have a much more low-level curiosity about my reactions than I have of yours –

> *SHE fastens her dressing gown a little tighter, then turns to dress.*

Why do you do that?

SHE: Do what?

HE: You always turn away from me when you get dressed like that.

> *SHE shrugs, pulls on her clothes.*

You are very uncurious about how you respond in a physical sense.

> *SHE pulls the blinds up. HE disappears into the bathroom.*

(Calling out.) You're very interested in humidity, pressure, wind, temperature – all those things.

> *SHE makes the bed throughout whilst he gets dressed in the bathroom.*

(Calling out.) But you aren't very interested in tastes – food, alcohol etc. You drink, eat without feeling… Pleasure even –

SHE: Yes. If I'm bored.

> *HE pokes his head around the door.*

HE: You're bored?

SHE: No. Yes. At times.

HE: You didn't enjoy what we just did?

SHE: It was fine.

HE comes back in.

HE: It was fine? *(Beat.)* You're not a sensualist.

SHE: *The deepest sensuality is the search for truth.*

HE: Don't quote DH Lawrence. I hate it when you quote Lawrence. It's so 50s. You have a part in this. You might be interested to know that in telling me what you would like I can take it… It will not reduce my power. In telling me *your* fantasy –

HE goes back into the bathroom to resume dressing.

SHE: No…not fantasy. I want unexpectedness. I don't tell you what I like because if I do… Let me put it another way… In the past, when I have, I have known men who as soon as they find out something works, grinds away at it the next night and the next, thus arousing in me an almost motherly concern for the pathos of the act.

HE comes back out now dressed.

HE: This conversation has come out of my gift to you of a sex toy.

SHE: Not only because of your gift to me… But because I think it is interesting what you think women want.

HE: I thought I was being modern in giving you a vibrator. You didn't even open it.

HE holds up the half-open package.

SHE: One of the difficulties of the vibrator is that your own hand is operating it. It's difficult to feel mystery in your own hand.

HE: Exactly. That is why I gave you an alternative. To your own hand. Your own finger.

SHE: A model of your dick? That's really very thoughtful, very kind. Something to keep me occupied…When you're not here. The penis is absolute king.

HE: I've begged you to educate me, and you find that very difficult. You won't just say, 'Hey, now, here's what I want you to do.'

SHE: I've talked to you, and you don't change. Much.

HE: The only reason I don't change is that I don't understand what you're telling me.

HE resumes dressing.

There are rituals when I come here.

SHE: Yes there are.

HE: I fly in. You pick me up. I drive. We get home.

SHE: You missed out a bit.

HE looks at her.

HE: *Occasionally* you satisfy me as I drive. We get home. Sometimes we eat. Not always. But if we do…after you hand me a towel. I swim then shower and then we make love. It's what you've come to expect.

SHE: Yes.

HE: And yet you ask for mystery even though most times you prefer the well-rehearsed plan.

SHE: No. You do. I don't ask for mystery because that's not part of the deal. If it happens in sex then great. With you it doesn't happen. Nothing is unexpected.

HE: Why unexpectedness in this area of your life and no other?

SHE: You want to do the same thing over and over again? I can't explain it. I don't ask to be moved to tears *every* time

I hear Pachelbel or 'The Butcher Boy'. It seems to me certain rituals are deeply comforting, even sensual.

HE: So it is pleasurable?

SHE: But constantly repeating?

HE: With you it's not boredom that's the problem; it's your lack of curiosity. About yourself.

> *SHE turns, looks at him – laughs.*

You hypothesise about men but you don't know what you like yourself.

> *HE pulls on the last of his clothes.*

It's not easy to arouse you. And I would say that's the purpose. I thought this way… This way. You could practise on your own.

SHE: Aiming for orgasm is a great burden. I will give you a book.

> *SHE stands, searches along the shelf for a book.*

There is a very good book on this I will give you to read.

HE: Please don't.

> *SHE takes out a book triumphant, searching through it.*

SHE: I know why I am doing it.

HE: Because *I* want it?

SHE: Yes. And that is the terms of our contract.

HE: What – you never have an orgasm?

SHE: Not never. Just not always.

HE: How many times have you orgasmed? I mean on average… When you do it… When we do it… When… with me?

SHE: You're a man who prepares for every trip.

HE fastens his watch strap, combs his hair, checks his wallet etc.

We're going on a drive. You want to know where we are going and how long it will take us to get there. But it's a nice automobile. We could take any road, arrive at any town, any time, find that we have no place to stay. That's fun. There could be a thunderstorm, we could have stomach aches –

HE: You're avoiding my question.

SHE: The road? The journey? I take my time. Don't always go the same route. I often wish I wasn't that way. With men the journey is usually the same from A to B. I wish I could jump into that with the same fervour and excitement. I am not saying you always do but –

HE: But I do.

SHE: You as a man will have an orgasm even if it is unsatisfactory. Even if it is boring. Any time. Any place. With anyone. *(Beat.)* The porn video tape is every frat boy's favourite side order now. Apparently. Or so my daughter tells me.

HE: A told you this?

SHE: She did.

HE: You talk about these things with your daughter?

SHE: She tells me a little. All the boys at college want the girls to do it like porn stars now.

HE: No kidding.

SHE: I have tried to talk to her with regard to the obvious exploitation of women. She's not remotely interested. *(Beat.)* She's dating a banker. Did I say?

HE: I thought he was a college boy.

SHE: He is a college boy… But he is going to be a banker. One day. Let's call him P. He calls her 'babe' a lot when he's not talking about the place he has just acquired at MIT. They came for lunch. He didn't ask me a single question.

HE: Why would he? You're just her mother.

SHE: There was a time…in certain cultures…there was a time…*is* a time in certain cultures, the mother was…*is* a goddess.

HE: Where is…was…this time…place?

SHE: I forget.

> *SHE drinks her coffee, checks her watch.*

She wants to move. To be close to him.

> *SHE wavers, looks back out of the window.*

Why are there workmen in my garden?

> *HE reaches for his coffee, drinks.*

HE: In Friday's *Men in Love*, the men want the women more than the women want the men. They want to be the instrument of the woman's pleasure. They will bind themselves with marriage, children and early death and keep trying.

SHE: You read Nancy Friday?

HE: I read the intro –

SHE: Really, why are there workmen in my garden?

HE: I'm having an irrigation system put in for you.

> *SHE looks at him, crosses the room, pours herself more coffee.*

For the record, I would rather make love to you, than with anyone else.

> *SHE hesitates, throws a half wave, through the glass.*

Because the pleasure I gain is not general. It is specific to the pleasure you give me. I give you. I hope. I thought I give you. From time to time.

SHE looks at him.

I would rather make love to you than to anyone else.

SHE drinks her coffee.

We have been together this year…73 days now. 73 days I have spent directly with you.

SHE: You know this for a fact?

HE: I do.

SHE: Do you tell your friend from Seattle, the same sort of thing?

HE: She's from Vancouver. Actually. *(Speaking into tape recorder.)* For the record.

SHE: Really? A Canadian?

HE: Yes.

SHE: She's Canadian. Does she like Canada?

HE: She must do. *(Beat.)* She's gone back to live there.

SHE looks at him.

SHE: Oh. I see.

SHE looks back out of the window.

You shouldn't have done that. I like watering. I go out in the evening and splash about a bit with the watering can.

SHE pulls on her dress.

HE: The Yucca was looking dry.

SHE: That is why I have a hose.

HE: I know. I told Julio to fix a hook so you could coil it.

37

SHE: I don't need an irrigation system.

HE: This way you don't have to think about it.

SHE: I don't want an irrigation system.

HE: You'll thank me.

SHE: It's my house.

HE: Which I pay for.

SHE: Which *I* pay for. From my earnings.

HE: It's only –

SHE: I don't want a *fucking* irrigation system.

HE: Right. Right.

> *SHE finishes dressing.*

SHE: There are ground rules. We've been over this –

HE: OK. OK.

SHE: …You visit. You don't put up hooks. You certainly don't organise workmen.

HE: I see.

SHE: My group… My group will be here soon. I'd rather they didn't see you.

HE: Fine.

> *HE pulls on his jacket, drinks his coffee.*

But just to be clear, I would rather make love to you, than with anyone else.

And no, I don't…didn't…say that to my friend, formerly of Seattle, now clarified as from Vancouver. Where she now lives. Where she has now returned to. Not to return to me. The pleasure that I am talking of occurs when you and I… When I make love to you.

SHE stands, a moment passes.

SHE: Well thank you. I hope you go on feeling that way.

HE: So do I. It's a very pleasant way to feel. I'd like it if you could feel it too.

SHE: My point is –

HE: I'll tell them to stop.

HE makes to go outside.

I gave you a vibrator because I thought it might be… something for you to try. It cost five dollars. Just dump it if you don't want it. Ball it into the trash.

HE goes to pick up the vibrator. SHE makes to stop him.

SHE: When we first met…the very first time we met at college you played with women.

HE: We were students.

SHE: I'd watch you controlling them, moving them in and then moving on, and not letting them in. It would have taken me a great deal of courage to receive a man, to take on a man like that…you… And to tell him *'Well what pleases me more? What upsets me when you do that is?'* So –

HE: You married someone else.

SHE: Then someone else again.

SHE hesitates. He looks at her.

And then when we met again. Even then if I had said *'It would please me more if you made love to me that way.'* You would have walked straight out of that hotel room. You would have gone, left, kept walking, pretended we'd never met again.

HE: I would not.

SHE: You would. It didn't matter. It was all very pleasing to me at the time. It was a relief… Really a relief from the hell… just a living hell. I was only just surviving… Just putting one foot in front of the other. Trying to hold it all together. I was…really…the eye…right in the eye…I was in the storm then with C.

I was mess… Really… A mess.

HE: And now?

SHE: And now these conversations are a real luxury –

HE: A psychic luxury. They come after we've ceased to be parents. Active mothers and fathers. Husbands…wives. So now you have the time… To ask yourself –

HE leaves the vibrator in her hand.

…what gives you pleasure now?

HE makes to exit through the window.

At least let me get you a goat. For that poison oak.

SHE laughs.

SHE: *(Calling after.)* It's a desert masquerading as a garden.

HE exits through the window. SHE looks down at the vibrator, takes it fully out of its box. SHE presses the button. It whirs. SHE hurriedly turns it off. SHE clocks the recorder. SHE presses rewind listening over the end of their conversation –

(From tape recorder.) It's a desert masquerading as a garden.

The doorbell rings again –

SHE hurries to tidy up, make the bed, hide HE's things, heading towards the door.

(Calling out.) I'm coming… I'm coming… Shit… Sorry… I've just got to… I'm here.

HE comes back in, looks at the audience.

HE: *(Direct to audience.)* I would like to point out that I don't always come off as well as I would like in the tapes. And listening again… I would like to think…listening again… one could detect a man struggling to hear, to see his own limitations.

> *HE turns, listening to distant voices. HE reaches for his coat, his briefcase.*

And to understand hers.

> *HE exits.*

SCENE 3 – POST CANYON RUN

SHE enters carrying groceries.

HE: What time do they get in?

> *HE stands steaming, post run, still in running gear. SHE glares at him. HE shrugs, pulls off his running shoes.*

SHE: Five.

> *Beyond the garden is taking shape, more cared for now, luscious plants growing. HE picks up a towel, rubs his hair.*

They're going to drive themselves from the airport.

> *It is lunchtime, 1987.*
>
> *A tape recorder rests on the counter.*

HE: Are you excited?

SHE: That my daughter's getting married?

> *SHE hands him a newspaper.*

No. Not at all.

> *HE quickly reads.*

HE: Damn.

> *SHE looks at him.*

When the top five are caught by the balls we're all in the soup… That's what happens when you let the young guns fuck it up running riot with their fucking fuck fuck back door computer fucking trading.

> *HE hurriedly folds it, moves on.*

SHE: How was your run?

HE: I stumbled. Right along the Canyon.

> *SHE reaches for a pen, writing on the back of a new tape box.*

Post Canyon Run. That is not a good title.

SHE: Ssh.

HE: These headings. These headings you write on the boxes –

> *SHE slides a new tape out of a tape box and into the recorder, pressing record. SHE presses record.*

SHE: They locate where we were in conversation. The locale. *Bed. Dinner at Hilary's. Ride in Car. Willow's Restaurant, Honolulu.*

HE: *(Direct to audience.)* We barely spoke in Honolulu.

SHE: *(Direct to audience.)* No… No… That's not true. There are two.

> *SHE searches along a shelf of tapes, pulling down tapes, reading alone each tape box spine.*

(Direct to audience.) No three tapes from that trip alone.

HE: *(Direct to audience.)* We drank. We drank a lot.

SHE: *(Direct to audience.)* He drank more. You talked a lot.

HE: I don't know how interesting we were that entire week. You didn't like the hotel much.

SHE: You are very lucid about climbing ropes in grade school. It lead to a good conversation with regard to masturbation.

HE: It did?

SHE: I would never have known that you enjoyed yourself so much in the Chinese Gambling houses.

> *HE picks up random things, packing them into his briefcase as if preparing to leave.*

What time's your flight?

> *HE exits to change.*

HE: *(Calling back.)* Five.

SHE: Did he say this was 1987?

> *SHE sorts through some more tapes, adding them to the shelf. HE comes back through, pulling on a clean shirt.*

HE: We won't listen to them.

SHE: Excuse me.

HE: Do you honestly think there will be a time when we listen to any of these tapes again?

SHE: I do. When we're older. When this is complete.

HE: When this is complete?

SHE: When this experiment is complete. We may wish to reflect. We may be asked to reflect. By our publisher. For our book.

HE: For our book?

> *HE laughs.*

God you're serious.

> *SHE smiles.*

So that the young might understand – see how we communicated… How we looked?

SHE: My thought would be the young are already doing this. Doing what we are doing. Talking like this. Or so I hope they are.

HE: I don't agree.

> *SHE stands, drags the sliding glass doors of the window open –*

I find them much less articulate than our generation.

> *SHE pours coffee.*

They tend to be muddle headed. I question whether they have a sufficient understanding of the language to carry out an adequate dialogue. You cannot think if you cannot express your thought. They can feel, but they cannot *think*.

SHE: Poppycock.

HE: Young people couldn't do this.

SHE: Then this will be a contribution to understanding what our mature years can make.

SHE checks the tape recorder.

HE: Will they even care? Do A and P ever talk like this?

SHE: I don't know. I don't know if they talk.

HE: Well I hope they do. Do you think P's seen this today?

HE holds up the newspaper.

Your daughter better be ready to work after they're married. No one is safe now. Not even P.

SHE: She wants a $25,000 wedding because it's traditional and says further that I should pay for it in order to prove to her that I love her. My response is to back off and wait for the next news. If your son told you that, and you didn't have $25,000, what would you say?

HE: I'd suggest a $10 wedding. Every wedding I've ever had has cost $10.

SHE: We had agreed to a period of non-communication. And then she calls. She wants money. We don't mesh with each other. Everything I say to her starts her emotions boiling.

HE: $25,000 dollars.

SHE considers her groceries, holding them up.

SHE: Steak or fish?

HE: Huh?

SHE: What would they prefer? Steak or fish?

HE: I don't know.

SHE: Just say. Steak or fish?

HE: Steak. No…fish.

SHE: I find it very depressing. That she is doing it. That she is getting married. I thought…I hoped she would want more. She'll marry and she'll want to work and then she'll have children and then the husband comes home and he wants sport. She'll be exhausted. And then what will P do?

HE: Bar prostitution.

    SHE hesitates, looks at him.

SHE: Prostitution is degrading for everyone.

HE: But there is an argument that in order to ensure men and women do live together, can survive together then a society that provides houses of prostitution and all sorts of things which a feminist would say is degrading even inhuman do, in fact, protect a large portion of females.

SHE: From what?

HE: From that responsibility to make love to their husbands. If they're *exhausted.* It's called society maintenance.

SHE: Society maintenance?

HE: What is the male to do if he is sensitive to the female and she says, 'For the next five years, I don't want to screw you'.

SHE: She doesn't say that. He isn't Torwald. This isn't the *Doll's House.*

HE: How is a man supposed to achieve physical satisfaction for those five years?

SHE: Assuming that males are totally different from females and they *must* have it.

HE: Listen at thirty… And that's when most men are siring children…at thirty…if I couldn't screw five times a day –

SHE: *(Direct to audience.)* Five times a day! *(To him.)* When you said that last time –

HE: That's right. I would have gone out of my goddamn mind.

SHE: Maybe you belong in an insane asylum. That's ridiculous. No wonder you didn't do anything significant until you were forty. How long were each of the five?

HE: Maybe fifteen minutes. One time could be thirty minutes or an hour.

SHE: Congratulations. Did the woman like it? I'm assuming they all rose up and said 'Bravo'.

HE: I'm merely reporting. You want this to be a candid exchange don't you?

SHE: I'm glad I met you again at 42 and not before. I couldn't think of anything more tedious than spending that much time not walking…not sleeping –

HE: In the depth of night you're not going to be out walking. Five times isn't very much.

SHE: Five times is monstrously much.

HE: You do it once when you get home. You do it three times in the night. You do it once in the morning.

SHE: Oh God…

HE: Well am I to tell you I didn't want to screw five times a day?

SHE: No.

HE: It just seemed normal to me.

> *SHE slides a dish into an oven.*

I don't think I was extreme.

SHE slams the oven door.

SHE: I think you were extreme. I think you're braggin'. So does Sally and her roommates.

HE: You told Sally?

SHE: I had dinner with her and them last week. She had Samuel for the weekend. God he's sweet. I was wondering whether I could be a spokesman for feminism when I had just read a lot of books and then I said 'Suppose when you were a nursing mother and your husband wanted it five time a night'. And they all screamed 'Five times a night?' 'Let him masturbate' 'Tell him it's abnormal' 'That sounds like service at a pump. 'And little Samuel had his chin on the table, his ears growing out like soup bowls, eyes darting from woman to woman. And I thought 'Now you…You are going to be different…Samuel…You are privy to so much…'

I use them as a sounding board as a check against our rampant theorizing.

HE: Most thoughtful, thinking men don't have that characteristic? Wanting to screw all day? And if women, aka you, don't want to be screwed by men, aka me, why are they, aka you, so attracted to them, aka me?

SHE: God you remind of my eldest. He said to me… I remember he once said to me 'Mom, I don't like big-breasted women. They just like me.'

HE: So you are the innocent victim?

SHE: If you're going to turn around now and call it an attraction –

HE: An attraction?

SHE: …between the women who like to declare periods of celibacy and men who like to screw five times a day.

HE: There lies the paradigm of male-female conflict.

Silence –

The payment for sexual services is degrading?

SHE: What we are…what this is…it's not that –

HE: Because we don't meet in a brothel?

SHE: It's different.

HE: Because I'm sensitive? Because I don't abuse you?

> *SHE gestures for him to be silent, straining to tune in the radio – listening to the murmur of the news.*

It's not that. What we are… It's not that.

> *HE resumes packing the last of his things.*

This gives us freedom. It helps that we can afford this. It's not available to most couples either psychologically or economically. How is a young couple to survive? I don't see how they can unless they make a dark and evil pact such as we have.

> *SHE makes to go. HE stops her.*

I haven't got $25,000 dollars. I'm sorry.

SHE: I was just telling you. I was just saying…

HE: I haven't got it.

SHE: No. I wasn't asking.

HE: Things are not good out there. At the moment, I'm struggling just to –

SHE: I wasn't asking. I have some of my own money that I have accrued, over the years. From my 'earnings' –

HE: Don't be like that.

SHE: I hoped for A it would be different.

HE: Of course it will be different. Just perhaps not in the way we imagined.

HE makes to go. SHE stops him.

SHE: Will we grow tired of one another like a husband and wife?

HE: I would hope not. *(Beat.)* I have to go –

SHE: You could stay another night.

HE: I can't. I have to be back. I've made plans.

SHE busies herself.

SHE: OK. I'll drive you. Let me just get this fish in –

HE makes to go.

If it would help… If you would find it easier… You can leave payment this month.

HE shakes his head.

HE: It's a bad spell. It'll pass.

SHE: I'm just saying.

HE: It'll pass.

SHE nods.

SHE: Are you being picked up the other side?

HE hesitates, looks at her.

HE: Yes.

SHE nods.

SHE: Right.

HE stops.

HE: A book? You really think this…all of this could be a book?

SHE: There might be something in it.

HE: I could –

SHE nods. SHE reaches for her keys, her purse.

SHE: Sure.

HE exits. SHE hesitates.

You don't want to miss that flight.

The radio murmurs on.

SHE: *(Direct to audience.)* It was 1974. Nixon had just resigned. I was clearing out the garage. C had taken the kids to the movies. I can't remember which movie. We were engaged in the increasingly familiar state of hostile silence. I was broken in every number of ways. I was hurrying to finish up. I had a yard sale of our life together spread out across the front lawn and I was working out the mechanics of how I get it into my car and down to the thrift store and back before he brought them home. It was hot. 102 in the shade. There were people passing out dead on their front porches from the heat. I was thirsty. I needed a drink. But mentally I was consoling myself, looking out at across the junk of our lives that I least...at least I was going to be rid of all of this...*stuff*... That at least I wasn't going to grow old with any of it...with anyone...I promised myself a cold beer if I finished by five. I had my mind very much on other things. So that when I first saw him, just getting out of his car, standing across the street, I didn't recognise him at first. And then he looked at me. It took a heartbeat. I thought if he crosses the street...

A car horn. SHE picks up her bag, goes to exit.

SCENE 4 – DINNER

The same low slung beautiful 60s house in West California now strung with blinds. There are books. Chairs. Tapes running along a shelf. A bed. A table. A typewriter. The sense the house now lived in, though this will progress throughout.

It is early evening, 1995.

HE stands a drink in hand, reading an article in a magazine.

The murmur of the TV underscores – Bill Clinton playing sax on the Arsenio Hall Show just audible.

His briefcase is open, paperwork out across a table.

SHE stands still wearing her coat.

HE: I let myself in.

> *HE hurriedly flicks the TV off. SHE puts down her handbag. HE holds up the article.*

So heterosexual sex is unnatural? The true order of things is sex between lesbians because of the early bond between mothers and daughters. Sally must be so proud of her article… Two pages. So what do males do? I don't know. I guess they just wander around in the ozone. I suppose they ejaculate into a spoon or something.

> *HE drinks.*

SHE: How much have you drunk?

> *HE smiles.*

HE: I've been here an hour already.

SHE: Really.

> *HE shrugs, pours himself another whisky.*

HE: It's for therapeutic reasons. My knee… My knee is playing up.

> *SHE takes off her coat.*

Where were you?

SHE: I drove down to the beach. I love to watch the changes in
the ocean. I thought you weren't getting in until late.

> *HE holds up a bottle of whisky, offering it. SHE shakes her
> head.*

SHE: There's a bottle of wine I started at dinner last night.

> *HE nods. She goes over, takes out an open bottle of wine,
> pours herself a glass. They chink. His hand touches her cheek.*

HE: You're cold.

> *SHE moves away.*

It's Friday. I always get the 3pm flight on Friday. So I'm
here by six.

SHE: Not every week.

HE: Most weeks. We've been doing this –

SHE: I'm just saying.

HE: We have been doing this forever.

> *SHE pulls away, goes over to the radio, tunes it to some music.*

SHE: Have you taken your shower?

HE: Not yet.

> *HE loosens his tie, resumes reading the article*

(*Reading article.*) According to Sally every child if she could
would fuck her mother.

> *SHE flicks the tape recorder on.*

SHE: That is, as ever, a very limited reading of it. However I
would say that there's a big difference between bonding
with your mother, because of one's physical closeness
to her, and sleeping with her. Never did I have a sexual
fantasy about my mother. I didn't even want to hug her

because of her corsets. Nor did I want to sleep with my father. I liked dogs and soft cats and horses.

HE: You had a tendency toward bestiality…

SHE looks at him.

Haven't we moved past this now? I was listening for a while back there…but now…

SHE: Well someone has to keep the lamp lit.

HE: Sally should ask herself whether her theories, would now let her produce her very beautiful child, my friend Samuel.

SHE: That's what the spoon is for.

Who, incidentally would like to thank you very much for that long board you sent him. Although Sally is convinced he will kill himself. He's ridden to school on it nearly every single day.

SHE drinks.

He wants to join the army.

HE laughs.

Are you going to be irritating all night? Because if you are I would prefer it if you got back on that plane. Had dinner somewhere else. *With* someone else.

HE: You're scratchy this evening.

SHE pours herself another glass of wine.

SHE: I couldn't sleep last night. I had a real headache.

HE: Did you take anything?

SHE: No. Not last night.

HE: Are you OK?

SHE shrugs, crosses the room.

SHE: I got up. Posted some letters and a parcel for little A. It's her birthday Friday.

HE: Already? I thought it was her birthday last time they visited. You took her to Disney –

SHE: It was. I did. It was horrible. I hate that place. That was a year ago. So that makes her now six. And little P, seven.

SHE drinks.

Are you hungry?

HE: What were you thinking?

SHE: Burnt lamb.

HE: Delicious.

SHE: I made it last night and left it under the grill too long but it tastes fine.

HE: Maybe later.

They drink.

SHE: I want to tell you something that happened.

SHE goes over, checks the tape.

HE: You want it on tape?

SHE: Yes, because I wonder if it's something that only happens to women, I wonder if what I am about to tell you happens to a man. It's probably solely a female experience.

HE: Like childbirth or suckling?

SHE: This happens after childbirth years. Long after that. Now.

HE: There is no such thing as the male menopause.

SHE: If I am wrong tell me.

SHE sits. Stands.

I have this friend, let's call him J, for the tape. He teaches out at the school. I only go in part time but… I mean I am barely there but when I am… I told you about him.

HE: No.

SHE: He's a musician, twenty-five years old, and it happens that he and I are capable of talking about a lot of issues and we merely tolerate the rest of the folks out of school. He's a graduate in art history. He's lively, funny, interested in a lot of things. I have mentioned him.

HE: You've never mentioned him before.

SHE: He's been at the school a while. I drive him home, whenever I'm in.

HE: Every time?

SHE: Most times. We've been out once or twice. We had lunch together at the bistro. That was fun. He showed me a song he had written and was sending to a publisher. We're always glad to see each other. He comes from divorced parents. His mother lives with an artist on the East coast. He's clearly very fond of his mother.

HE: The scene is set.

HE sinks down into a chair.

SHE: He took me to his house, where he lives with several people and he took me next door to introduce me to his musical group. They were sweet…nice people. So we exchange favours, and he's been wanting to come see my castle.

HE: Here?

SHE nods.

SHE: I feel at ease with him. I enjoy being with him. I like talking to him. It's not like talking to a feminist, where there's a skirmish going on at all times. He understands all that.

HE: You told him about us?

SHE nods.

SHE: So in return for showing me his dwelling, he came out here.

HE: And you cooked him lamb.

HE nods. SHE goes over checks the tape is still playing, resting on a side table close by.

It was a beautiful evening and so after we took a walk along the ridge and we were nattering away, talking about things we talk about. We had been discussing what he does when he's not playing in groups and I asked 'Do you have a woman in your life?' We were walking down the trail. It's really hard to tell this. And he said, 'The only woman I think about is the woman who's walking down the trail in front of me.' I didn't say anything. 'You're supposed to stop and say something pregnant.'

HE laughs.

And I said 'That's only in stories and TV' and I kept on walking. We walked on the road down below and then he said 'May I kiss you?' and I said no.

HE gets up, pours himself another whisky, drinks.

HE: Go on.

SHE: And we got up to the steps outside the front and he said 'What I am trying to say to you is that I am very much attracted to you, and I'd like to sleep with you.' And I said… I can't remember what I said. I must have indicated 'No'. And here's why I am telling you. I thought about why I was absolutely certain that the answer was no. Oh, one of them things I told him was that I had done this before once, with a twenty-five-year-old –

HE: When? When we were together?

SHE: No… Yes… Just before…possibly after… I can't remember…if we were together. I can't recall. And now it's happened again and I am a lot older and there comes a time of retirement. And I know that I am in it. I knew in that moment I was in it. 'Have I made you very uncomfortable?' and I said 'Yes you have.' So much so that today –

HE: Today?

SHE: Yes… So much so that I didn't go to school today, because I knew he would be there.

HE: Right.

SHE: Is there anything in a man's life like that? Where you think 'I'm a certain age and I can't do that again?'

HE: Yes –

> *HE drinks, gets up and goes over to a drinks cabinet, fills up his glass.*

It happens to me lots of times – when I think 'No, I don't have to do that… Work it like the younger guys… Swagger in the bar after the gym… Try to impress clients… I'm the President of this fuckin' company. I'm past having to do that.'

SHE: No, I mean that you're too old. That you can't. Because you're too old.

> *HE stands, drinks.*

HE: I don't like to think of it as growing old. The dividends that come from both of us having been through most of life's experiences –

SHE: Do you know what you are about to do, in feminist terms?

HE: What?

SHE: Give one of your lectures.

HE: Well, I might be giving one of my lectures, but our ability to take these arguments to as far as I can see, totally absurd conclusions –

SHE: It's like Tinker Bell coming into Peter Pan's life over and over again – just when he thinks he's got things going well with the Darling family, then Tinker Bell comes in with her jealousy. This conflict asserts itself in the most idyllic circumstances and causes conversations to begin in one place and dart off into strange, dangerous canyons.

> *HE slams his drink down.*

HE: You know I'm not going to go through anymore Sturm and Drang with you anymore. We either live peacefully or not at all. I've had it.

> *SHE interrupts him.*

SHE: The reason for my response to J is age.

HE: What?

SHE: My age.

HE: You're not so damn old.

SHE: Why are you so angry?

HE: You've got those feelings about your body… Your mastectomy… You've got these feelings about your mastectomy.

SHE: I'm asking you, would you have done that? Would you have?

HE: If a twenty-five-year-old wanted to fuck me?

> *SHE nods.*

No. No. I would have fucked her back.

SHE: That's what I thought.

> *SHE nods, crosses the room.*

HE: You need to talk about your mastectomy. On the tape.

SHE washes up her glass, puts it away.

SHE: I would like to postpone a discussion of this until the day after tomorrow, at eight o'clock please. The reason why I would like to postpone it is that it tilts, weighs, skews. It confuses the whole picture. Makes our talks Pollock rather than Munch or Van Gogh.

HE laughs.

It makes us look stranger than we might otherwise.

HE: I don't understand.

SHE: We want the woman in this book to have a quality of every woman –

HE: Aged over –

SHE: *(Cutting him off.)* Thank you again. To give me a mastectomy robs me of that everywoman quality.

HE: Why?

SHE: Because few women have mastectomies.

HE: That's not true.

SHE: What? One in ten thousand?

HE: Betty Ford. Shirley Temple, Ingrid Bergman had two. Happy Rockefeller – two.

SHE: You know this stuff? That is a very strange roll call to be able to just reel off.

HE: I looked it up. When you…when you…when it became obvious that you were going to have it… When it happened. I looked it up. I find mastectomies are no more than any other physical signs of decay. Like wrinkles and fat deposits and varicose veins. I put it all in the same category. We're coming apart at the seams…literally.

SHE: I'm thinking of the reader. It's disconcerting thinking of someone with one breast.

HE: I don't think that's true. It might be true for females but for males it's…ho hum.

SHE: You're being gallant.

HE: Being in good physical shape that's what matters. Then again it is conceivable if I didn't have a penis or lost my balls, I would feel the same way. But breasts aren't primary sexual organs.

SHE: Some men regard them as primary. It makes her odd. It makes her mathematically odd.

HE: That is odd.

SHE: Plus it means explaining. The effect it has had. On her.

> *HE wavers, looks at her, she picks up a watering can, tweaks at plants.*

It's a loss. No matter what people say, how positive the world is, how many positive thoughts one is meant to have – it is a loss. Women keep a stiff upper lip and men are gallant. I know of no published negative comment by a man on the effect of it. And yet I *know* they think them.

HE: But breasts just plain old ordinary breasts, by the time most women are fifty…

SHE: Mine are just the same.

HE: Your one is.

> *SHE crosses the room over to the tape recorder, goes to change the tape.*

SHE: I don't like this tape.

> *HE stops her.*

HE: It's a good tape…

SHE concedes.

If you had the choice of large pendulous decayed breasts or –

SHE: I'd rather have one.

HE: So you'd rather have one small breast than two large pendulous ones.

SHE: Yes… Particularly if they were decayed.

HE: If you had two breasts you would still be as body shy as you are now.

SHE: Not as much. I think of the pre-mastectomy period as relative abandonment compared to what I feel now.

HE: You don't want the reader to feel sorry for you.

SHE: Are they still together because she had a mastectomy? Is the mistress-master contract possibly like a slum redevelopment project?

HE: I think that's why you didn't screw J. *(Beat.)* If it was, then you should know it doesn't make a difference. It doesn't make a difference to me. It wouldn't to any man. I find you interesting and I love to screw you.

SHE: It might also be the case you are being noble and virtuous. I cost too much, I'm hard to get along with sometimes. You might find another woman. You might have found another woman since…

HE: The first night we slept together… After…post-operative… you constructed that sash… And what did I say to you…

   Silence.

I said 'Take it off.'

   Silence.

Look at me.

SHE hesitates, turns to look at him.

'Take it off now. I want you not the goddamn sash!'

SHE: And I had to comply. You can do anything you want with me.

HE shakes his head, releases her.

Why are you so angry?

HE: Because I don't want you to fuck anyone else.

SHE reaches out a hand, stops him.

Because I don't want to fuck anyone else.

SHE: I dreamt last night that you turned away from me to another woman who gave you what you need, want, and can use. I thought we should call this off –

HE: I don't want any other woman.

SHE: I could only watch the transfer and weep.

Sometimes if you're not here and I am alone I have to go out until I know you will arrive.

They look at one another.

Sometimes my fear is so dense it becomes my weather, my element.

The tape plays on –

HE exits. SHE turns, faces the audience –

SHE: *(Direct to audience.)* I talked to my daughter on the phone last night. A. She's doing very well. Really. I'm very proud of her. She has a very, very important job. Which she likes me to console her over. I tell her she works too hard. She barely gets time with her kids. They have a nanny which helps. I tell her they'll be flown soon. Five…ten more years and it'll just be her and P. And she says 'Oh Christ…Mother please no.' But they're very

63

wedded to one another. I don't lecture. I listen. As my
mother did not. She favours the pant suit. For work. I tell
her 'My generation fought for you to take your place at
the boardroom, Sweetheart.' She's very disinterested in
feminism. Ever since Clinton marched with the feminists in
'92 she says our work is done. I see a chink of light in Little
A. I'm working on her. She'll be finishing college soon. A
still picks up her husband's socks. P's socks. I tell her she
needs to stop that right away. 'Mom...what I'm in is no
different to what you are in. We're both in marriages of a
kind.' I disagreed. Mine can be ended at lightning speed.
Hers... He will take her for every penny she has. He's a
teacher now. He doesn't earn so much. They are both in
a way mutually trapped. But I went to the library anyway.
To verify her assertion. I tried to find actual marriage
codes. What I was able to get aplenty are the various state
grounds for divorce. If she refuses sex, it is grounds for
divorce. Also the husband's failure to provide doctors,
food, dwelling, enough money to run the household. I
must tell A that. She really doesn't know her rights at all.
And then I realised the difference was I have a choice. No
church. No state has locked me in...bound me in marriage
to anyone.

SCENE 5 PRE-BREAKFAST

The low slung, house –

SHE sits, in the half light, in her nightdress and robe.

It is dawn, 2010.

HE enters in his robe half reading a piece of paper.

HE: There are three 'ns' in cunnilingus.

SHE: *(Direct to audience.)* It is dawn, 2010.

> *SHE looks at him.*

What time is it?

> *SHE peers at her watch.*

SHE: Five. Nearly five.

HE: Did anything come through on the fax?

SHE: *(Shakes head.)* It's not yet 8 in New York. His office won't be open yet. I was just looking over the proposal I sent him. I'm still unsure about a couple of the chapters. I'm going with the names on the tapes.

> *HE looks over her shoulder, reading the papers in front of her.*

HE: *Bed. Conversation at Hilary's. Willow's Restaurant, Honolulu. Post cinema. Telephone.*

SHE: They're clear. You can't say they're not clear.

> *HE and SHE face the audience.*

HE: *(Direct to audience.)* When our publisher received the proposal by fax from –

SHE: *(Direct to audience.)* R.

HE: *(Direct to audience.)* When R received the proposal by fax which had subsequently been scanned through by his assistant to his Blackberry, R was with his wife about to go to see the Menil collection.

SHE: *(Direct to audience.)* That's in Houston Texas.

> *SHE turns to HE.*

We need an initial for his wife.

> *SHE turns back to the audience, smiles.*

(Direct to audience.) I've always liked the thought that R and his wife –

HE: T –

SHE: Really? T – ?

(Direct to audience.) …that R and T walked around that collection straight after. I suffused it with the thought that R was thinking of us as he took in all those beautiful artifacts. A collection built by the Menil's over thirty years of their marriage.

HE: *(Direct to audience.)* Mr and Mrs Menil were French but moved to Houston during the Second World War.

SHE: They can work that out for themselves, Sweetheart.

(Direct to audience.) I liked the symmetry. That R and T were looking at possibly one of the greatest art collections and here we are offering them another collection…a collection of artifacts of sorts. Both born from very different marriages, of course.

HE: *(Direct to audience.)* Though you would never call this art.

SHE: *(Direct to audience.)* No… Of course not. This is not art… But truthful… I want it to be truthful. It has to be truthful. It is our life after all.

> *He turns to her.*

HE: It will be.

SHE: You can't be sure. It's all open to interpretation.

> *She turns to look at the audience.*

(Direct to audience.) But the most important point is that I –

> *He looks at her.*

That we wanted to leave something behind. To prove –

HE: *(Direct to audience.)* …our existence.

SHE: No…no.

HE: *(Direct to audience.)* …to bring our story…into the modern world. To show that two of the pathetic, screwed-up generation had endured.

> *SHE looks at him.*

SHE: *(Direct to audience.)* To show we had endured.

> *HE reads on.*

HE: In general your spelling is appalling.

SHE: Do you want coffee?

> *SHE crosses the room, pours herself some coffee.*

HE: No. It'll keep me awake. You know if you had typed it on to a computer it might have been easier.

> *SHE goes to take the paper from him.*

SHE: May I have it?

> *HE moves across the room, holding the paper, towards a desk.*

HE: Do you have any Tipex?

SHE: Second drawer. It doesn't matter now. He's already got it. I faxed it pretty much straight away. He said he would let us know by the end of the day. But I waited up late and nothing… Nothing… I thought he might have called but there was no message on the answer phone so… Perhaps he'll just fax his answer back.

HE: The title's a little obvious.

SHE: R likes it.

HE: He does?

SHE: It's what will sell it. He says it is what will sell it. He says it does what it says on the can. He's a publisher. He should know.

> *SHE runs a finger along a row of tiny cassettes, one of several rows of cassettes lining the walls.*

And then I thought perhaps we should have sent him a tape or two. With the proposal.

> *SHE keeps searching along the row of tapes, craning her head to read various dates and titles.*

HE: You barely punctuate.

SHE: I'll do it. Give me the page.

> *SHE crosses the room, holds out her hand.*

HE: Nobody…nobody writes on a manual typewriter anymore.

SHE: I do.

HE: It's the 21st century.

SHE: It's quicker. More immediate. It's very easy to change a word –

HE: Yes, it's called spellcheck.

SHE: With a pencil. Computers are often temperamental. They go kerplunk!

HE: Then you buy another. And sending him the proposal by fax? He will think you a dinosaur.

SHE: I liked the connection. To its past. To the first time.

HE: *(Beat.)* You are a romantic.

SHE: I oppose the dictatorship of objects. You have a computer. You are a slave to it. With a typewriter the only screen is the paper and your mind. Do you think I should have faxed it on headed notepaper?

68

HE: You type then fax a proposal and you're worried it's not on headed notepaper? What it is proposing… It's our story he is interested in. Not headed notepaper. And it's a very persuasive method in your hands. Enticement by fax.

> *SHE looks at him. He resumes correcting. SHE crosses over, reaches for a coffee pot, makes coffee.*

Why do you think he will want to listen to the tapes?

SHE: To authenticate. To ensure we haven't made it up.

HE: Who would bother making it up?

SHE: Someone. People who want to make money.

HE: There must be easier ways.

SHE: *(Direct to audience.)* People write about their lives, the tragedies of their lives. There was that guy, that guy…said he'd been in a concentration camp, when he hadn't. He was praised for his chapter on rats eating his feet. And it was all a lie.

HE: *(Direct to audience.)* Wilkomirski.

SHE: That was it…That was it…

HE: It was on *Oprah*.

SHE: When do you watch *Oprah*?

HE: When you're out. If I was early and you're weren't here… I used to… When I came over and you weren't in… I watched *Oprah*…

SHE: Right.

HE: Though *Ellen* is –

SHE: You watch *Ellen*?

HE: …From time to time.

SHE: We won't be on *Oprah*. We didn't do it to be on *Oprah*.

HE: *Ellen.* We could be on *Ellen.*

SHE: Will people think we've done it – ?

HE: If we did go on *Ellen* –

SHE: Which we're not.

HE: No. I'm just saying…if we came out and wanted to be on *Ellen*… Our story is the kind of story that she would do.

SHE: That is the joy of anonymity.

HE: It is.

SHE: By the time it comes out we'll be dust.

HE: If we had wanted to make money from this –

SHE: *(Direct to audience.)* That's not why we did this. For money. We wanted to see if it was possible. *I* did it because I was broke. Broken. I'd been screwed around by fathers, husbands, lovers, judges and I didn't want to be screwed around anymore. I was out of the woods. My feminism got me out of the woods. But how was I to live now? Because I wanted to love men again. With all my feminism in my hands, I wanted to see if I could love men again.

> *SHE crosses the room.*

Although the advance would not go amiss. If he goes for it.

HE: It's a good deal.

SHE: Exactly.

> *SHE hesitates.*

Did you hear something?

HE: No. Open the door. You should open the office door that way we'll hear it. If it comes through… On the fax.

> *SHE nods, exits. He reads over the paper, correcting a little more. SHE enters.*

SHE: I opened the door.

HE: Good.

SHE: Nothing yet.

> HE nods. SHE nods. SHE drinks her coffee.

I mean what better way to end.

HE: *'What better way to end?'*   .

SHE: This experiment. What better way to complete this experiment?

HE: Experiment.

SHE: To conclude this arrangement? It can come to its end now.

HE: I don't understand.

SHE: Because it's served its purpose.

HE: Its purpose.

SHE: It's given us both what we wanted, what is more important, what we needed.

HE: Yes.

SHE: It seems the natural point to punctuate.

> *Distant sprinklers –*

Damn. The sprinklers shouldn't come on until six.

HE: I set them earlier. It was very dry so I set them earlier.

> *SHE goes over to the window, peers out.*

SHE: When did you do that?

HE: When I was last over. Friday… When I was over Friday. I could see… It was cracking… You have to change the dial. It'll stay on longer then.

SHE: I can do that.

HE: No you can't. If you had you would have seen that the Yucca is wilting. Again. Though how anyone wilts a Yucca. They have survived over cultivation, two world wars and various fungus since 1753 –

SHE: I'll hose it down later.

HE: You can't. The hose is cracked. Because you didn't coil it. You don't coil it. It gets frost this time of the year. Then you step on it and it cracks. I told you last year and you didn't listen... I went and bought you a new one. You've done the same with it. There used to be a hook.

SHE: It rusted.

HE: So I set the sprinklers again. That is what an irrigation system is for.

> *HE crosses the room, pours himself a drink. SHE tidies up the papers, desk around her, putting back tapes onto shelves.*

SHE: You know if you give yourself some time to adjust to it, it's not as daunting as it might seem. Nothing will really change. We are friends of course. But with this book. The financial side... Well I would hope the financial side... I will be fine so... I'm dissolving our agreement.

> *Suddenly the long low sound of a fax –*

> *They listen until the sound stops – the fax arrived.*

HE: I guess his office is open now.

> *SHE goes to exit.*

I'll get it.

> *SHE hesitates, nods. HE exits. SHE busies herself, goes to pour herself more coffee, drinks, waits. HE enters, holding a piece of paper.*

HE: He's not convinced.

> *SHE stops.*

SHE: What?

HE: R thinks we stopped too early. He thinks there's a couple more chapters still to be written. A conversation still to be had.

SHE: He said that?

HE: He says he is concerned as a proposal it might be 'a little thin.'

> *SHE crosses over to read the paper. HE snatches it away from her. SHE starts to take down tapes from the shelves.*

SHE: Well we could pad it out. There's a lot I left out. I didn't put in that whole period when you were having problems with your son. When he came to work for you. And… Oh my God and there is that whole month when we did not get out of bed in that little house we stayed up in Napa… I didn't put that in because I was worried it was getting a little weird… That was a weird week… We drank way way too much and I seemed to remember there was quite a lot of smoking involved. And then there was the diet period after I got sick… When we were starving ourselves, literally starving ourselves.

> *HE reaches for a notebook, searches the pages.*

HE: *(Reads.)* We spent 179 days together that year. 2 less than we have so far this year…181 days this year.

> *SHE hesitates, rifles through some papers.*

SHE: It was gobbledygook when I listened over to it again. It must have been the drugs I was on after my surgery. We were hypoglycemic most of the time we were so hungry… I left that whole period out… But there's some good stuff. I could… I could…pull some stuff out from there. 181 days. I didn't know you still kept a record.

HE: Yes.

SHE: What – you have written down how many days we have
spent together every year?

HE: Yes.

SHE: I didn't know you still did that.

HE: I like to get my money's worth.

SHE: Don't be indignant? Really. Now you wish to be
indignant?

> *SHE goes over to a shelf, fingers tracing along a shelf of tapes –*

If it's too short – I didn't transcript half of what I found.

> *SHE rifles through a sheaf of papers, reading.*

HE: There is certainly stuff you have left out.

SHE: *(Direct to audience.)* Often… Often when you listen to our
conversation…we are very repetitive… *(To HE.)* You in
particular… The early 90s you got very…elliptical. Really
the conversations often went nowhere… You should listen
over them again.

> *SHE looks over the shelves of tapes.*

HE: Then it is as much about what we leave out as what we put
in? This book?

> *SHE looks over the tapes, reading the spines of the tape boxes.*

'You're dissolving our agreement?'

SHE: That was always the deal. Under the terms of the
contract. Either party may conclude it. I mean we didn't
expect it to go on forever now did we.

HE: Right.

SHE: I was always very clear.

HE: Yes.

SHE: The terms were very clear.

HE: Yes.

> *SHE reaches over, takes down a new tape. HE takes it, peels off the wrapper, puts it into the tape recorder, presses record.*

If this is published, don't believe *He* and *She* will keep the world at bay. Someone will come and find us. Someone will want to interview us. To understand why we have done what we've done… Perhaps someone will want to make it into a movie.

SHE: You've been watching too much *Ellen*.

HE: People will ask why we did what we did.

SHE: Then they can read the book. Watch the movie.

HE: Then they'll warp it. Because they weren't there. And we won't be there to tell them otherwise. And they won't know. Other than what we have given them and the rest… the rest they'll surmise…create. From what we don't say.

SHE: And – ?

HE: And it won't be about us anymore. And just for the record… It's a contract. Not an agreement. You don't dissolve a contract. You break a contract. We made a contract. You're breaking a contract. It was never an agreement.

> *He leans over the recorder.*

For the record.

> *Silence.*

HE: The primary scarcity that we have is time. Every moment you spend on one thing has an opportunity a… cost… when you could be doing something else.

SHE: It sounds frantic, the way you put it.

HE: It's not frantic. It's philosophical.

SHE: You're rambling now.

HE looks at her.

HE: Last night… After we ate dinner and we drank some wine. And then, my sweet lady, forgive the expression, you fucked me. In the way we have come to enjoy.

SHE: I don't forgive the expression. I made love to you, and if I remember rightly, I had to stop your talk with kisses. You never used to be so talky in bed. In fact, that was part of your magic, that you said nothing.

HE: Quite inappropriately, you continued with your plans. I had no choice.

SHE: To save you the trouble of pointing it out, I controlled the lovemaking and enjoyed every minute.

They look at one another.

I wanted it.

HE: And now you want to end it? Our time together, you want to end?

SHE: We have thirty years of output. *(Clasping the paper.)* Right here. Don't you want to share that? Let the personal become political. The thought that someone will read this…discuss this…what we have done… Doesn't that mean something?

HE: What for a book? Another book? For another fucking book?

SHE: Yes.

HE: For your sisters? For Sally? For our activist Sally so she can stomp and shout and march on for the fucking cause? Can we just agree – this private fucked-up gender war is over now? The battle is over. There is no battle now.

Your words. Your words.

She looks at him.

SHE: Did I really say that? Well that was a ridiculous thing to say.

Really? I didn't really say that?

The battle can never be over.

We've always got to shout.

Otherwise what has any of this been for if but idle conversation – ?

HE: No one should ever start an idle conversation with you. It's like pursuing a cyclone.

SHE: Good – you're listening.

> *They look at one another.*

HE: *(Beat.)* Has it ever occurred to you that men and women will never be equal? That nature will always tip the balance. That the primal will always outweigh any attempts the sexes make to find a new kind of equality and that the only thing that keeps us equal…keeps us vigilant is this discourse. That when we stop talking that is when we're lost.

> *HE hesitates, hands her the faxed paper. SHE looks at him then looks down at the paper. SHE looks up.*

SHE: That's –

HE: Incredible.

SHE: He liked it.

> *HE hesitates, nods.*

HE: Yes.

> *HE nods, turns his back on her.*

SHE: You lied to me.

HE: Yes.

SHE: He asked us to sign it straight away.

HE: I should ask my lawyer to go over it…

> *HE searches for a pen.*

There was a pen somewhere.

> *HE finds one, turns to hand it to her.*

SHE: Your name's first.

> *HE hesitates, signs. SHE takes the pen, signs. They look at one another. HE turns to go.*

We'll need new tape.

> *HE looks at her. SHE crosses the room. HE catches her hand.*

Second drawer.

> *HE nods, releases her. SHE crosses the room, pours coffee. HE searches, finds a tape, slides it into the tape recorder, presses record. HE looks at her, then leans close to the tape –*

HE: She and He first met in graduate school in the 1950s. When they met again, nearly twenty years later, they began an affair. From the beginning, they were frank and honest with each other; it was, after all, an enlightened, postwar world.

> *SHE crosses the room to him, coffee in hand.*

SHE: Following a phone conversation that had made her unhappy about all of this, she had a bold idea. A 'CONTRACT'. It proposed a unique set of terms for their relationship.

> *SHE hands him the cup of coffee, he drinks.*

HE: The terms of the agreement have been in force for over thirty years. They never had any children together, but –

SHE: *(Direct to audience.)* They now have several grandchildren between them.